BOARD GAMES

With Price Guide

Desi Scarpone

Schiffer Publishing Ltd

77 Lower Valley Road, Atglen, PA 19310

DEDICATION

This book is dedicated to my mother, father, brothers and sister for providing me with the happy childhood that I am constantly trying to recapture.

Library of Congress Cataloging-in-Publication Data
Scarpone, Desi
    Board Games: with price guide/Desi Scarpone.
      p. cm.
    Includes bibliographical references and index.
    ISBN 0-88740-725-0 (soft)
    1. Board games--Prices--United States--Catalogs. 2. Board
      games--United States--History--20th century. I. Title
    GV1312.S33 1995
    794--dc20   94-36469
                      CIP

Printed in Hong Kong.
ISBN: 0-88740-725-0

Published by Schiffer Publishing, Ltd.
77 Lower Valley Road
Atglen, PA 19310
Please write for a free catalog.
This book may be purchased from the publisher.
Please include $2.95 postage.
Try your bookstore first.

We are interested in hearing from authors with book ideas on related subjects.

Contents

Acknowledgments

Thanks are due to a variety of people who contributed to the creation of this book:

Gene Trindl for his photographic skills,

Kathryn Gutzmann of Minnesota for her excellent research into Schaper Manufacturing,

Carol Yamanoha, Grace Tanaka and Ronda Berkeley for their input and support,

and Hub Braden, without whose help I literally could not have done this book.

Thanks go to Bill Bruegman who provided photos of some of his games from TOY SCOUTS, INC., an excellent source of Baby Boomer toys and games. A catalog can be obtained by writing Bill at 137 Casterton Ave., Akron, Ohio 44303 or calling him at (216) 836-0668.

I am deeply indebted to Jeff Lowe who took the time to photograph a couple hundred games from his huge personal collection. Jeff sells games as well, and a catalog can be yours by writing to him at 5005 Tamara Lane, West Des Moines, Iowa 50265 or calling him at (515) 226-9404.

Special thanks go to Rick Polizzi, his long suffering wife Carla and "Pickle," for the many photographs he provided and the fascinating look into his wonderful collection. Rick co-authored the excellent book *Spin Again* featuring "Board Games from the Fifties and Sixties," and publishes a spin-off of his book, cleverly titled *Spin Again*, a snazzy newsletter "celebrating the world of Toys, Games & Collectibles." Rick can be reached at 3400 Greenfield Ave. #7, Los Angeles, CA 90034 or by phone at (310) 559-4866.

Most of all, my thanks go to Peter Schiffer for giving me a chance to do a book like this.

Introduction

There have been thousands of games manufactured over the years from the early 1800s to the present. This book offers an overview of the continuing popularity of board games. In addition, over 1000 color photographs of games and an estimate of their current market value will be offered for each.

Games exist on many levels. Certainly as art in many cases, and as a reflection of our society in others. Games have been a focal point of family entertainment in many households, and with the advent of television, an extension of them in thousands more. It is no accident that a multitude of games were emblazoned with the phrase "As Seen On TV." The fact that we could bring home a piece of what we saw on television allowed us to participate more fully in the total experience. We could match wits with game show hosts on their own turf (and maybe beat them at their own game), or continue our favorite space hero's adventures long after they had disappeared from the T.V. screen. Most board games were designed to enable children to compete against mom and dad on an equal basis, and that inspired the kids with confidence, or at the very least, a competitive spirit. Games were even the center of many a feud between friends and family, usually over someone's interpretation of the rules. Everything managed to come out alright in the end, though. After all, you couldn't alienate *too* many of your buddies because every kid had a game at *their* house you wanted to play!

The games in this book were selected to be representative of as many board games as possible. Besides being fun to look at and reminisce, it is an invaluable reference guide to the approximate values of the games. The time period covered is generally from the 1940s to the 1970s, although a few will be from an earlier or later period.

I have tried to divide the games into distinctly different categories; yet many games could easily fall into any of several categories and my placement of them is purely arbitrary. I have followed the evolution of a particular game through its cover art whenever I could, such as Milton Bradley's CHUTES AND LADDERS (showing the various covers from 1940 through the 1960s that reflect art styles or themes of the time) or shown variations of the same game in different incarnations, such as Parker Brother's ever popular MONOPOLY, on which there is a separate chapter. When possible I have tried to show the complete series of a theme of games, such as Hasbro's monster mystery games of the 1960s, or Milton Bradley's American Heritage series. In addition, there is a chapter on W. H. Schaper, the man who created the plastic COOTIES game and other visually arresting diversions.

Through ignorance or sheer lack of space, much has been left out. Everyday I discover more games that I never knew existed. Also, I am constantly finding other games I remember from my youth and the feeling, to me at least, is of discovering a long lost friend. The joy and happy times associated with the game come flowing back from long-deserted corridors of my memory, and I feel contented that the game is back in my safekeeping. Maybe that's why people collect games; to remind them of the simpler, carefree times of their lives, or as an escape from the stresses of our daily adult struggle to survive. Then again, maybe people just like to play them.

Determining Values

The values of games, as with most collectibles, is a very strange mixture. The condition, scarcity, physical location, aesthetics, emotion, current game market trends and pure economics all contribute. The value ranges given in this book are for games that are from Near Mint to Mint condition, meaning games that are complete and look as though they never have been used. The ranges reflect prices you could get in various geographic locations and in various situations, but are by no means set in stone. Games that are still sealed in their original plastic wrapping are often worth much more than stated, yet games that look good but are missing essential pieces may be worth far less. The values listed in this book are only a guide. It will be up to you (the Buyer or the Seller) to determine what a fair price is for you.

You should start by checking whether the game is complete, and note any missing implements (including the directions). Imperfections like split corners, tears, water or tape damage to the box should be considered. The game's rarity and desirability should be a factor, although this can be misleading. One would think that because only a single game was made about The Beatles, (THE BEATLES "FLIP YOUR WIG" GAME by Milton Bradley, 1964), and taking into account the popularity of Beatles memorabilia, this game would be very rare. On the contrary, although desirable, the game is reasonably common (because a lot were manufactured) and the price usually reflects this fact. The asking price often leads many board games to languish on a dealer's shelf because it is not in line with the game's real value in today's marketplace. There is a big difference between a game's real and its perceived value.

In addition, age alone does not always determine a board game's value. There are games from the early 1900s that are common and undesirable, and consequently worth very little. Yet some games

from the 1970s are valuable because of a factor like low distribution, and they happen to become desirable. The combination of elements such as these sometimes make a game worth a seemingly disproportionate amount.

Once you have decided what is good or bad about the game, you (the buyer or seller) can factor in all these variables against what a "mint" copy of the game can be worth and determine pricing from there. The seller should not give the game away, but also he should not price it out of the market. Conversely, the buyer should not pay an outrageous price (which encourages the seller to continue high pricing) nor attempt to bargain the price down to a level which both parties know is unfair.

The majority of dealers and collectors with whom I have dealt over the years have been fair people. If they have not already acknowledged a flaw in a game they are selling, they are receptive when one is pointed out, and reduce the price accordingly. Most dealers will offer some kind of guarantee (especially if you are buying games through the mail where estimates of condition can be diverse) and refund your money if you are not satisfied.

Unfortunately, the following situation has happened to me many times and, as the proliferation of game price guides increases, will probably happen in the future: I approach a seller who has a game for sale. I ask how much they want for the game. They reach under the table and consult a price guide, proceeding to show me what the game is "worth". I explain to them that the top end price quoted in their book is for a game in mint condition and that their game is missing pieces or has several tears in the side panel, and therefore is not in mint condition. I even show them the grading chart in the front of the guide that affirms what I am saying.

Nevertheless, they stand firm in their resolve that their game is worth the high end price because "the book says so." I suppose the game will remain in their inventory until they understand that what "the book" says, and what the game's actual value is, are two very different things.

It takes only one "wild card" to wreck the situation. Although I stress that this book is just a guide in pricing, and many variables make up a value, if one person comes up and says "I'll take it" regardless of the price or condition, that price becomes the game's new value. Reality and price guides go right out the window. And that's the game of collecting!

DISCLAIMER

The prices listed for games in this book are approximations and are based on the author's personal experience. They are formatted from a variety of sources including flea markets, swap meets, catalogs, game lists, toy shows and collectible conventions. There are many different factors that contribute to a seller's asking price (such as condition, scarcity or geographic location, etc.) but only one factor that determines what a game is worth: what the buyer is willing to pay. With that in mind, neither the author nor the publisher can be held responsible for any fiscal losses that occur through the use of this book in the purchase or sale of games.

Chapter 1

Western and Military

Games associated with the wild west have always been popular through the years, but especially proliferated during the 1950s and 1960s, mainly as a result of the media influence of movies and television. Although board games based on western personalities from radio (such as Parker Brother's THE LONE RANGER) had been around since the 1930s, Milton Bradley's THE HOPALONG CASSIDY GAME was one of the first board games based on a television personality, and others swiftly followed. The Davy Crockett craze was in full force during the mid 1950s and many westerns came and went. Transogram's THE WILD, WILD WEST GAME was based on the show of the same name which crossbred a western theme with the spy craze of the 1960s. However, by the late 1960s, westerns on television and their game counterparts had reached their end and slowly faded out, replaced by the myriad other offerings of the electronic medium in the 1970s.

Generic games based on the strategy of war and warfare, whether modern conflicts or ancient skirmishes, have consistently plied the imagination of young and old alike. Like western games, they have been popular for many years. Almost no real war has been too repugnant to have a game based upon it (with the possible exception of the Vietnam conflict) and the games associated with them usually have a patriotic fervor about them. Countless games have resulted from World War I and especially World War II, but once again it took television to produce the shows that resulted in a preponderance of games that appeared in the 1960s. Although games like Ideal's COMBAT and Transogram's McHALE'S NAVY were fun, other games existed that were not based on popular entertainment and required a lot of strategic thought. Games that challenged the imagination included Parker Brother's RISK, Milton Bradley's SUMMIT, and Games Research's DIPLOMACY. These games often lasted for hours, if not days, with the inevitable goal of world domination through armed aggression or stealthy negotiation.

The following are a few examples of Western and Military games:

WELLS FARGO GAME
Milton Bradley 1959
T.V. series starring
Dale Robertson
$25

BRANDED GAME
Milton Bradley 1966
T.V. series starring Chuck Connors
$25

JOHNNY RINGO GAME
Transogram 1960
$25-40

GENE AUTRY'S DUDE RANCH GAME
Built Rite 1956
includes stock car race game
$15-20

HOLD UP ON THE OVERLAND TRAIL GAME
Transogram 1960
T.V. series starring William Bendix
and Doug McClure
$40-50
Courtesy of Toy Scouts, Inc.

STAGECOACH WEST ADVENTURE GAME
Transogram 1961
T.V. series starring Richard Eyer,
Wayne Rogers and Robert Bray
$25-35

GUNSMOKE
Lowell 1958
T.V. series starring James Arness
$35-55

JACE PEARSON'S TALES OF THE TEXAS RANGERS
All-Fair 1956
T.V. series starring Willard Parker
and Harry Lauter.
$35-45
Courtesy of Rick Polizzi.

BANDIT TRAIL GAME FEATURING GENE AUTRY
Kenton Hardware Co 1950's
scarce game
$55-75
From the collection of Jeffrey Lowe.

THE CATTLEMEN
Selchow/Righter 1977
Western strategy game
$10

WAGON TRAIN
Milton Bradley 1960
T.V. series starring Ward Bond,
Robert Horton
$20-25
Courtesy of Toy Scouts, Inc.

MAIL RUN
Quality Games 1960
Based on obscure T.V. series
"PONY EXPRESS"
$30-40

HAVE GUN WILL TRAVEL
Parker Brothers 1959
T.V. series starring Richard Boone
$25-35

HOPALONG CASSIDY GAME
Milton Bradley 1950
Very early T.V. series starring
William Boyd
$45-55
Courtesy of Rick Polizzi.

BAT MASTERSON
Lowell 1958
T.V. series starring Gene Barry
Sets up similar to GUNSMOKE
$35-45

JOHNNY RINGO GAME
Transogram 1960
"Round up the Rustlers with Johnny Ringo!"
CBS T.V. series starring Dan Durant as Johnny
Ringo and Mark Goddard as Cully, better known
as Don West in LOST IN SPACE.

THE GAME OF PONY EXPRESS
Polygon Corp 1947
$20-25
From the collection of Jeffrey Lowe.

THE FASTEST GUN
Milton Bradley 1974
large, 3-D game
$15-20

COWBOY ROUNDUP GAME
Parker Brothers 1952
$12

THE RIFLEMAN GAME
Milton Bradley 1959
Imagine the thrill kids got when
they discovered they did not help
Lucas (Chuck Connors) shoot bad
guys as the cover suggests, but
instead help round up cattle.
$30-35

DOC HOLLIDAY WILD WEST GAME
Transogram 1960
$20-25
Courtesy of Toy Scouts, Inc.

STRAIGHT ARROW
Selchow & Righter 1950
Based on the radio program
$25-30

11

THE FESS PARKER TRAIL BLAZERS GAME
Milton Bradley 1964
from the Daniel Boone T.V. show
$25-35
From the collection of Jeffrey Lowe.

WALT DISNEY'S OFFICIAL DAVY CROCKETT RESCUE RACE
Gabriel 1955
Fess Parker as Davy Crockett
with real compass
$25-35
Courtesy of Rick Polizzi.

FRONTIER FORT RESCUE RACE
Gabriel 1956
same game, no Davy Crockett
with real compass
$20-25

CHEYENNE GAME
Milton Bradley 1958
T.V. series starring Clint Walker
He was replaced by Ty Hardin for a
period and a cover exists with his image.
$25-30

CHEYENNE GAME
Milton Bradley 1958
Uncommon- from a "Rainy
Day Fun" series-Clint Walker on cover
$25-35
Courtesy of Toy Scouts, Inc.

SHOTGUN SLADE GAME
Milton Bradley 1960
T.V. series starring
Scott Brady
$20

THE LONE RANGER GAME
Parker Brothers 1938
Separate board and box
from the radio show
$55-65

THE LONE RANGER GAME
Milton Bradley 1966
Based on cartoon series
$15-20

THE LEGEND OF THE LONE RANGER GAME
Milton Bradley 1980
Based on movie
$10

RODEO THE WILD WEST GAME
Whitman 1957
Comes with illustrated story
of the western rodeo
$10-15
From the collection of Jeffrey Lowe.

THE LONE RANGER GAME
Parker Brothers 1938
Full size box edition
from radio show
Hi-Yo-o-o-o-o Silver!
$45-55

BUCKAROO THE COWBOY ROUNDUP GAME
Milton Bradley 1947
$20-25
From the collection of Jeffrey Lowe.

ANNIE OAKLEY GAME
Milton Bradley 1958
Western personality
$20
Courtesy of Rick Polizzi.

COMBAT!
Ideal 1963
"The Fighting Infantry Game"
T.V. series starring Vic Morrow
and Rick Jason
$20-25

COMBAT! CARD GAME
Milton Bradley 1964
$15

BATTLE LINE GAME
Ideal 1964
Based on the T.V. series
$20-25

12 O'CLOCK HIGH GAME
Ideal 1965
T.V. series starring Robert Lansing.
Another cover exists depicting
Paul Burke
$30-35
Courtesy of Rick Polizzi.

PURSUIT!
Aurora 1973
World War I flying ace
game- Don Adams on cover
$15-20

12 O'CLOCK HIGH CARD GAME
Milton Bradley 1965
$15-20

CONFLICT
Parker Brothers 1940
Strategic War game
Metal pieces
$25-35
From the collection of Jeffrey Lowe.

CONFLICT
Parker Brothers 1960
$20-25

CONFLICT
Parker Brothers 1964
$15-20

TANK BATTLE GAME
Milton Bradley 1975
Elaborate game with miniature
tanks.
$20

COMBAT TANK GAME
Magic Wand 1964
4 magnetic tanks-
from a game series
$15-20
From the collection of Jeffrey Lowe.

TANK BATTLE GAME
Milton Bradley 1975
Slightly different cover
$20

SEA BATTLE
Lido Toy Company 1940s
Plastic ships
$20-25
From the collection of Jeffrey Lowe.

SEA BATTLE
Kaywood Corporation 1950s
Similar to BATTLESHIP
$18-25
From the collection of Jeffrey Lowe.

BLOCKCADE
Corey Games 1941
"A Game for Armchair Admirals"
Metal ships or cardboard cutouts
$25-30
From the collection of Jeffrey Lowe.

13

CHOPPER STRIKE
Milton Bradley 1976
"The Two Level Land/Air Battle Game"
Miniature plastic anti-aircraft guns
and helicopters make this unique
3-D game very attractive. Pieces
similar to TANK BATTLE GAME

P.T. BOAT 109
Ideal 1963
Plays like BATTLESHIP
$15-20

CONVOY THE NAVAL WAR GAME
Transogram 1960s
Plays like BATTLESHIP
$15-17
From the collection of Jeffrey Lowe.

CARRIER STRIKE!
Milton Bradley 1977
"A Game of Naval Strategy"
Big game with plastic Aircraft
Carriers and airplanes similar to
TANK BATTLE and CHOPPER STRIKE
$20-25

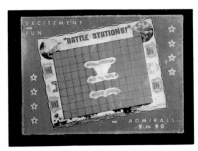

BATTLE STATIONS!
John E. Burleson 1952
Plays like STRATEGO
comes with sealed secret orders
"For 'Admirals' 9 to 90"
$25-30

GUIDED MISSILE NAVY GAME
Milton Bradley 1964
"Whirling Top Missile" scores
points
$12-15

20 TO 2
Dearborn Industries 1949
"A New Game Sensation for You
and You and You!" Scarce game
in which 20 pieces try to outwit 2
pieces and vice-versa
$20-25

STRATEGIC COMMAND GAME
Transogram 1962
Large game in which
"Magnetic Force is your Partner"
$25-35

ELECTRONIC RADAR SEARCH GAME
Ideal 1969
$15-20

SONAR SUB HUNT
Mattel 1961
"A Naval Battle Game"
Large game in which you use
Periscopes to sight enemy
subs and fire "torpedoes"
$35-45

SUB SEARCH GAME
Milton Bradley 1973
large 3 level, 3-D version
of BATTLESHIP
$20-27

SUB ATTACK GAME
Milton Bradley 1965
$15-20

RANGER COMMANDOS
Parker Brothers 1942
$25-35
From the collection of Jeffrey Lowe.

CHOPPER STRIKE
Milton Bradley 1976
$20-25

SUBMARINE CHASER
Milton Bradley 1939
Wood pieces
$25-35
From the collection of Jeffrey Lowe.

15

BLACKOUT
Milton Bradley 1939
$25-35
From the collection of Jeffrey Lowe

STRATEGY
Corey Games 1938
"The Game of Armies"
War God Mars on cover?
$25-35
From the collection of Jeffrey Lowe.

CAMELOT
Parker Brothers 1950s
"The Greatest of Modern Games"
$20

CAM
Parker Brothers 1949
"The Great Game"
Abbreviated version of CAMELOT
$20-25

LEGEND OF CAMELOT
Hoyle 1987
Lots of plastic Knights
$15-20

BLACKOUT
Milton Bradley 1939
Different version
$25-35
From the collection of Jeffrey Lowe.

STRATEGY
Corey Games 1945
Medieval cover but still
game of modern warfare
$20-25

CAMELOT
Parker Brothers 1961
$15-20

LEGEND OF CAMELOT
Hoyle 1987
Lots of plastic Knights
$15-20

VICTORY BOMBER
Whitman 1940s
Target game with wooden "bombs"
$20-25
From the collection of Jeffrey Lowe.

CAMELOT
Parker Brothers 1932
Popular Edition
Evolved from CHIVALRY, one of
games George S. Parker invented.
$20-25

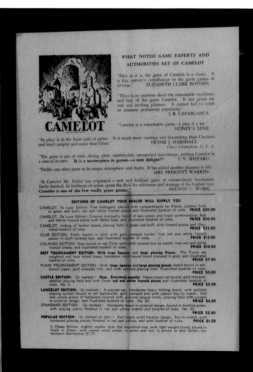

BATTLEBOARD
Ideal 1972
Pound an air pump and blast your
opponent's pieces off the game board
Similar to BLAST
$10-15

SWORDS AND SHIELDS
Milton Bradley 1970
$15-20

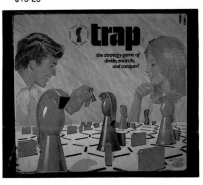

TRAP
Ideal 1972
Strategy game
$8-10

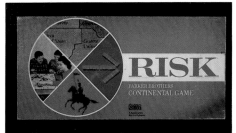

RISK!
Parker Brothers 1959
Original Edition
Take over the World!
Wood pieces, although some
early editions had plastic pieces
$10-15

RISK
Parker Brothers 1968
$7

PRINCE VALIANT
Transogram 1955
"A Game of Valor" based
on the strip by Hal Foster
$25-30
Courtesy of Rick Polizzi.

CITADEL
Parker Brothers 1940
Wood pieces
$25-35
From the Collection of Jeffrey Lowe

SUMMIT
Milton Bradley 1961
"Global Strategy" game
Reaction to the Cold War
$20

SIEGE GAME
Milton Bradley 1966
Plastic Knights
$20-25

PHALANX
Whitman 1964
Named after combat formation
$15-20

CONFRONTATION
Gamescience Corporation
World Strategy game came in a
envelope- Scarce
$20-25
From the collection of Jeffrey Lowe.

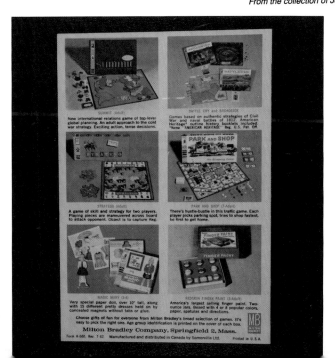

DARK TOWER
Milton Bradley 1981
Electronic game of Dragons and Wizards-
You attack and the Dark Tower
tells you how you fared.
$25-35

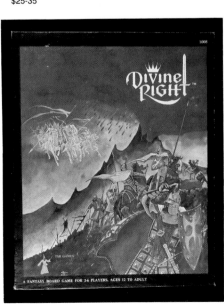

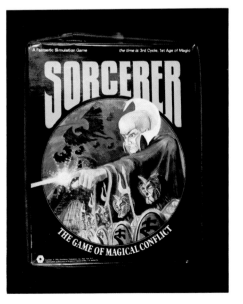

DUNGEONS & DRAGONS
Tactical Studies Rules 1974
"Original Collector's Edition"
One of the first role-playing games
$15-20

DIVINE RIGHT
TSR 1979
Role-playing game
$10

SORCERER
Simulations Publications Inc 1975
Early role-playing game
$10

MILITARY CHESS
Joseph Cossman & Co 1959
Military chess pieces with
battleground chess board
$10-15

COUP d' ETAT
Parker Brothers 1966
Card game with metal daggers
$10-12

THE FAMOUS GAME OF HALMA
Parker Brothers 1915
(shown without board)
Similar to CHINESE CHECKERS
$20

BATTLESHIP
Milton Bradley 1967
Updated version of old games
(a non-photographic cover exists)
$10

ELECTRONIC BATTLESHIP
Milton Bradley 1979
"Live Action and Sound"
Same series as DARK TOWER
$20-25

THE FAMOUS GAME OF HALMA
Parker Brothers 1938
$15

STRATEGO
Milton Bradley 1961
Original Edition
"Old World Game" with wood pieces
$15

STRATEGO
Milton Bradley 1962
Plastic pieces
$10

STRATEGO GAME
Milton Bradley 1960s
$10

CAMPAIGN!
Saalfield 1961
"The American 'Go' Game"
Civil War theme
$25-30
From the collection of Jeffrey Lowe.

CAMPAIGN
Waddington 1971
Napoleon era game
$15-20
From the collection of Jeffrey Lowe.

1863
Parker Brothers 1961
Civil War Game
"Created by the Editors of
LIFE Magazine"
Probably a reaction to Milton
Bradley's GAME OF THE CIVIL WAR
$15-20

AMERICAN NERITAGE GAME OF THE CIVIL WAR
Milton Bradley 1961
Command Decision Series
Civil war theme with plastic soldiers
$20-25

AMERICAN HERITAGE BATTLE-CRY
Milton Bradley 1961
Command Decision Series
Same as GAME OF THE CIVIL WAR
$20-25

AMERICAN HERITAGE BROADSIDE
Milton Bradley 1962
Command Decision Series
American Revolution Plastic ships
$20-25

AMERICAN HERITAGE HIT THE BEACH
Milton Bradley 1965
Command Decision Series
Plastic soldiers World War II
$20-25

AMERICAN HERITAGE DOGFIGHT
Milton Bradley 1962
Command Decision Series
Air Battle World War I
Plastic planes
$25-30

AMERICAN HERITAGE SKIRMISH
Milton Bradley 1975
American Revolution theme
Included in a re-issue of 1960's
American Heritage games
$15-20

G.I. JOE COMBAT INFANTRY! GAME
Hasbro 1964
Based on the doll
$20-25
Courtesy of Rick Polizzi.

G.I. JOE MARINE PARATROOP! GAME
Hasbro 1960's
Based on the doll
There was another game in the series
called G.I. JOE RIK-O-SHAY GAME and
G. I. JOE NAVY FROGMAN GAME
$ 20-25

G.I. JOE COMMANDO ATTACK GAME
Milton Bradley 1985
Based on cartoon series and action
figures-Large "gameboard"
$10

CONQUEST OF THE EMPIRE
Milton Bradley 1984
Gamemaster series
Complex game with a lot of plastic
pieces
$25-30

AXIS & ALLIES
Milton Bradley 1984
Gamemaster series
Tons of Plastic
Another game in series was
BROADSIDES & BOARDING PARTIES
$15-20

FORTRESS AMERICA
Milton Bradley 1986
Gamemaster series
Future theme- Popular because it had
Saddam Hussein as antagonist on cover
years before "Desert Storm"
$25-35

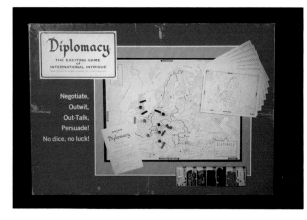

DIPLOMACY
Games Research Inc 1971
Original Edition
Negotiation game that could last
for hours or days
$20

DIPLOMACY
Games Research Inc 1971
$15-20

Chapter 2

Business, Book Shelf, and Sports

The idea of games dealing with "business" in the traditional sense has been around a long time, and here it's meaning has been stretched to include almost any type of game whose objective is to amass a fortune (or lose a fortune, as in the case of Selchow and Richter's GO FOR BROKE). Games based on the stock market have been popular, as well as games involving the importing or exporting of goods. But it really took Parker Brother's MONOPOLY to set the standard for finance games involving buying and selling, in this case real estate. Games of business allowed children and adults alike to earn a make-believe fortune that was often denied them in real life. Like arm-chair quarterbacks who second guess coaches from the safety of their homes, business games enabled everyone to prove they were savvy enough to play with the big boys. Or, as Transogram's BIG BUSINESS put it, "HOW SMART ARE YOU AT BUSINESS? HERE'S $150,000. PROVE IT!"

Bookshelf games were developed in the 1960s and are still being manufactured today. Basically, they are a small compact game with a board that folds up four ways (rather than in half) and implements that fit into a small box. This box then slides into a hard slipcover that has the name of the game and manufacturer printed on the spine, resembling a book. Many "volumes" were made, ranging from business games to medieval war games. When lined up on a shelf, they resembled a row of books, hence the name "bookshelf games". 3M and Hasbro made the bulk of these in the 1960s, but when Avalon Hill took over 3M they basically became the primary manufacturer of this type of game.

Games emulating sports have been enormously popular from the board game's very beginnings, especially when a popular icon of the era endorsed it. This section does not pretend to cover all the multitude of sports related games available, but it will give the reader a general overview. In broad terms, games associated with a particular player are more valuable. Some sports games, like Tudor's electric series, are very common. They were made in many variations for so long that all but the very earliest examples are virtually valueless, and as such are not included here. The same might be said for Cadaco-Ellis' "FOTO-ELECTRIC" series, if it weren't for their box covers. Like most early Cadaco-Ellis games, they were often quite beautiful. Even so, there are just too many of the "FOTO-ELECTRIC" games around to command much value.

...Play your own
9-hole course
using tips from the master!

© THE DAVID BREMSON CO., 1961. ALL RIGHTS RESERVED

LEARN GOOD GOLF IN THE LIVING ROOM

CONTROLLING INTEREST
American Greetings 1972
"The Business Game that
Corners the Market on Fun"
$15-20

MANAGEMENT
Avalon Hill 1960
Early business simulation
game
$15-20

FORTUNE 500 THE BUSINESS GAME
Pressman 1980
Elaborate business game
$20-25

THE MONEY GAME OF JUNIOR EXECUTIVE
Whitman 1960
Girls are always "Secretaries" to
the boys who are "Bosses"
$10

THE MONEY GAME OF JUNIOR EXECUTIVE
Whitman 1963
$10

GO FOR BROKE
Selchow & Righter 1965
Unusual game in which the object
is to lose all your money.
It's harder than you think.
$10-12

GAME OF BOOM OR BUST
Parker Brothers 1951
Perennial favorite
$20-24

BOOM OR BUST GAME
Parker Brothers 1959
$10-15

FINANCE AND FORTUNE
Parker Brothers 1936
Similar to MONOPOLY
$15-20

FINANCE AND FORTUNE
Parker Brothers 1936
$15-20

THE GAME OF FINANCE AND FORTUNE
Parker Brothers 1955
$10-15

FINANCE
Parker Brothers 1956
$5-7

EASY MONEY
Milton Bradley 1936
Similar to MONOPOLY
Patent issued by Parker Brothers
$15-18

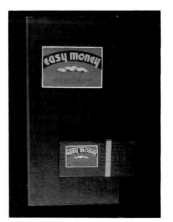

EASY MONEY
Milton Bradley 1936
$15

EASY MONEY
Milton Bradley 1940's
$15-20

23

EASY MONEY
Milton Bradley 1950's
$10-12

STOCK MARKET GAME
Whitman 1963
"The Aristocrat of Money Games"
Neat game
$10-12

SPECULATION STOCK MARKET GAME
Speculation 1969
$20

MONEY! MONEY! MONEY!
Whitman 1957
Talk about keeping up with
the Jones'
$15-20

BIG BUSINESS
Transogram 1937
(Board shown does not match game)
Transogram's answer to MONOPOLY
Debuted in 1936
$20-25

EASY MONEY GAME
Milton Bradley 1974
$5-7

STOCK MARKET GAME
Whitman 1968
Deluxe Edition
Harder to find
$15

TRANSACTION
John R. Tusson 1962
Mr. Tusson was "Searching for
the secrets of the Stock Market"
when he invented this game
$10-12

NEIMAN-MARCUS' TEXAS MILLIONAIRE
Texantics Unlimited 1953
Might have been a give-away
Contains "266 Million Bucks"
$15-22

BIG BUSINESS
Transogram 1954
Popular Edition
$10-12

ARBITRAGE
H.C. Jocoby Inc 1986
"Wall Street- Try it Before
You Risk it"
$5

TICKER TAPE
Cadaco 1963
Elaborate entry from "Mr. Fun"
$15-17

IN THE CHIPS
Tega 1980
Local investment game of the
Santa Clara Valley (Silicon Valley)
$7-10

WHITE GLOVE GIRL
American Publishing Corp 1966
"A Manpower Game"- Advertisment
for Employment Agency
$12-16
From the collection of Jeffrey Lowe.

THE FAMOUS BIG BUSINESS
Transogram 1959
Quality Edition
$10

BIG BOARD
Eskay Co 1975
"The Stock Exchange Game"
$12-15

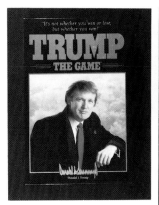

TRUMP THE GAME
Milton Bradley 1989
Based on Media Hypest
Donald Trump
$10

LUCKY TEN THE MONEY GAME
Lucky Ten Co 1974
$5

THE DINERS' CLUB CREDIT CARD GAME
Ideal 1961
Based on the Diners' Club
$25-30

DALLAS
Southfork Dallas Collection 1985
Based on the T.V. series
"Empire Building Strategy"
$10

BILLIONAIRE
Happy Hour Inc 1956
3-D Vacuformed Plastic
Uranium hunting
$20-25

BILLIONAIRE
Parker Brothers 1973
"Game of Global Enterprise"
Marvin Glass & Associates design
$10-15

B.T.O.
Bettye-B 1956
$20-25

ORGANIZED CRIME
Koplow Games 1974
Crime as "Business"
May have been inspired by
The Godfather Part II
$10-12

THE GODFATHER GAME
Family Games 1971
Original Edition came
in violin case. May have been
inspired by the novel- Scarce
$35-50

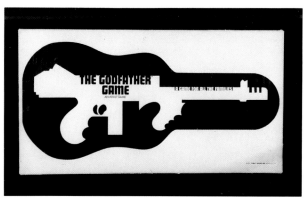

THE GODFATHER GAME
Family Games 1971
$7-10

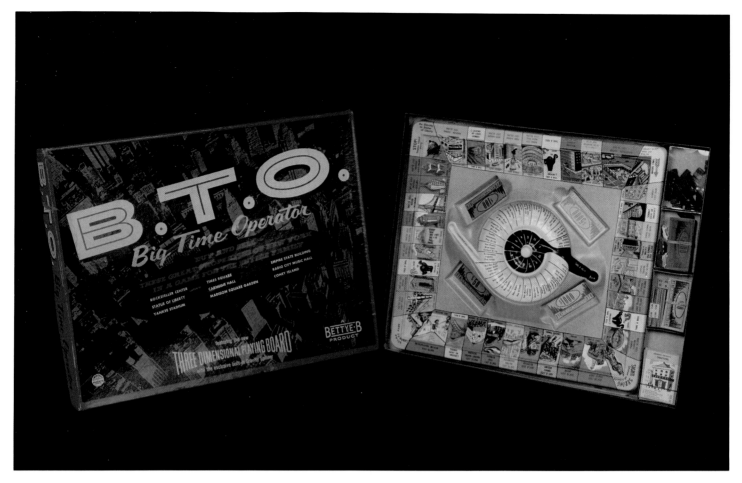

B.T.O.
Bettye-B 1956
"Big Time Operator" 3-D Vacuform Design
Buy and Sell properties like Carnegie Hall,
the Statue of Liberty and Coney Island

TYCOON
Parker Brothers 1966
$10-15
From the collection of Jeffrey Lowe.

CALL KELLY
Games For Industry 1966
Promotional game for Kelly Girls
"Temp" services
$10-15

TYCOON
Wattson Games 1976
"The Rags to Riches Game"
$5

BEVERLY HILLS
Tonguenchic Corp 1979
"A Game of Wealth & Status"
Shop at expensive stores on
Rodeo Drive
$10-17

HOT PROPERTY! THE BOARD GAME
Take One Games 1985
"Make the Deals that Make the Movies!"
Unusual packaging-came in film can
$20-25

RATRACE
Waddington 1970
"A Madcap Game of Social Climbing"
$8-12

SQUARE MILE
Milton Bradley 1962
"Land Development Game"
Take undeveloped land and
build cities
$20-25

PRIZE PROPERTY
Milton Bradley 1974
"The Land Development Game"
Basically 3-D version of
SQUARE MILE
$15-20

HOTELS
Milton Bradley 1987
Another 3-D game of land
development- into hotels
Very cool
$20

YANKEE TRADER
Corey Games 1941
"A Game of Trading Skill"
$20-27
From the collection of Jeffrey Lowe.

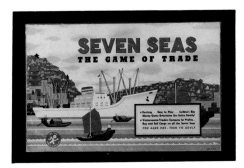

SEVEN SEAS
Cadaco 1960
"The Game of Trade"
$15-17

GAME OF EXPORTS AND TRANSPORTATION
Mills Games Mfg Co 1936
Narrow box full of trade cards
$15-20

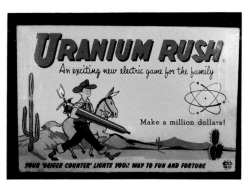

URANIUM RUSH
Gardner Games 1950's
"Geiger Counter" lights and buzzes
when you discover "Uranium"
Scarce
$75-125

URANIUM
Saalfield 1955
Another game about
"Uranium prospecting"
$15-25

KING OIL
Milton Bradley 1974
Great game where you drill
for "oil"
Plastic pieces
$15-20

GAME OF THE STATES
Milton Bradley 1954
Sell products coast to coast
Plastic cars- Common
$10-12

GAME OF THE STATES
Milton Bradley 1960
$8-10

GUSHER
Carrom Industries 1946
Great Grandfather of KING OIL
$25-35
From the collection of Jeffrey Lowe.

MANAGING YOUR MONEY
Cuna Mutual Insurance Society 1969
"Money and Insurance Game" offered
through Credit Unions
$7-9

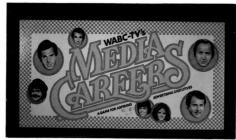

WABC-TV'S MEDIA CAREERS
ABC 1977
"A Game for Aspiring Advertising
Executives"- Promotional
Lists T.V. shows for that year
$10-15

PAY THE CASHIER
Gelles-Widmer Co 1957
Teaches you how to make
change "quickly and accurately"
$10-12

PARK AND SHOP
Milton Bradley 1950's
Before there were Malls
Popular game
$20-25

PARK AND SHOP
Milton Bradley 1960
"The Shopping Game"
$20

SHOPPING CENTER GAME
Whitman 1957
$10-12

SUPER MARKET
Selchow & Righter 1953
"The Red Light-Green Light Shopping
Game"
$22-25
From the collection of Jeffrey Lowe.

POP-UP STORE GAME
Milton Bradley 1950's
Board folds open to 3-D
store
$20-25
From the collection of Jeffrey Lowe.

ACME CHECKOUT GAME
Milton Bradley 1959
"The Exciting New Super-Market
Shopping Game"
$20-25
From the collection of Jeffrey Lowe.

INFLATION
Charles Joseph-Carpenter Game Products 1974
$5-7

TAXOLOGY
Gloria Game Co 1957
Taxpayers "Guide to Survival"
$10-15

MONEYPOWER
Sherman Games 1980
$5-7

MR. PRESIDENT
3M 1967
"The Game of Campaign Politics"
$10-15

QUINTO
3M 1969
Number game
$8-10

FEUDAL
3M 1969
Plastic Knights
$15-20

FOIL
3M 1969
Word game
$8-10

JUMPIN
3M 1964
Metal pawns
$8-10

BREAKTHRU
3M 1965
Strategy game
$10

PLOY
3M 1970
Future Strategy game
$7-9
From the collection of Jeffrey Lowe.

PHLOUNDER
3M 1962
Word game
$10-15
From the collection of Jeffrey Lowe.

FACTS IN FIVE
3M 1967
Trivia game
$7-9

HIGH BID
3M 1965
"The Auction Game"
$10-12

BAZAAR
3M 1967
"The Trading Game"
$7-9

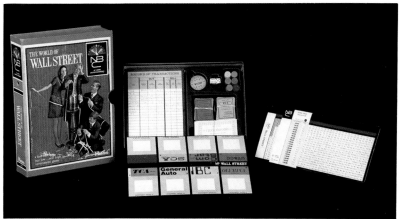

THE WORLD OF WALL STREET
Hasbro 1969
Part of a "At Home Entertainment" series
A changing "Market" made this a fast
paced exciting game

LIE CHEAT & STEAL
Reiss 1976
Flat box version of same game
$15-20
From the collection of Jeffrey Lowe.

LIE CHEAT & STEAL
Dynamic Games 1971
"The Game of Political Power"
A division of Reiss
$10-12

WHO CAN BEAT NIXON?
Dynamic Design 1970
$20-25

POINT OF LAW
3M 1972
Real cases are presented
and you decide how they
should have been resolved
$10

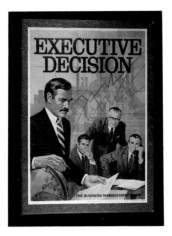

EXECUTIVE DECISION
3M 1971
Business management
$10-12

ACQUIRE
3M 1968
"High Adventure in the
World of High Finance"
$10-15

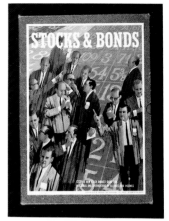

STOCKS & BONDS
3M 1964
Buy and sell as the
"Tote Board" changed
each turn
$10

THE WORLD OF WALL STREET
Hasbro 1969
$10-15

MOB STRATEGY
Hasbro 1969
Crime game
$10-12
From the collection of Jeffrey Lowe.

INTERPRETATION OF DREAMS
3M 1969
Came with "Dream Dictionary"
$15

IMAGE
3M 1972
Trivia game
$5-8

FOREIGN EXCHANGE
Avalon Hill 1979
"International Money Game"
$7

HIGH BID is the exciting auction game in which players try to complete valuable collections by outbidding and outbluffing their opponents. For 2 to 5 players. Bookshelf case contains game board, property cards, buyer's cards, special dice, play money and complete instructions. (GA-190)

JUMPIN is an absorbing game of pawns for 2 players or 2 teams. Each player attempts to be the first to get his pawns to the opposite side of the board by jumping over his own or competitor's pieces. Bookshelf case contains playing board, gold and silver pawns and instructions. (GA-150)

OH-WAH-REE is an ancient and absorbing pit-and-pebble game. Players capture pebbles by "sowing" pebbles from the most strategically located pit. For 2 to 4 players. Bookshelf case contains fold-away playing board, pebbles, pit markers and instruction folder. (GA-120)

PHLOUNDER is the action word game in which players race to build the right word and to be the first to ring the bell. Special dice allow children and adults to play together. For 2 to 6 players. Bookshelf case contains letter tiles, maze, bell, special dice, score pad and instructions. (GA-100)

QUINTO holds the fascination of numbers as each player attempts to obtain the highest score possible by playing up to five tiles totalling 5 or a multiple of 5 in a straight row. For 2 to 4 players. Bookshelf case contains playing board, multiles, number tiles, score-card, pencil and instructions. (GA-160)

STOCKS & BONDS lets each player buy and sell stocks and bonds as he tries to become the wealthiest player in the game. For 2 to 8 players. Bookshelf case contains Stock Board, chalk, eraser, dice, situation cards, stock certificates, calculator, record sheets and instructions. (GA-170)

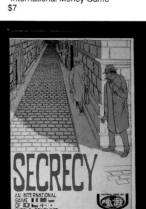

CREATURE FEATURES
Athol-Research Co 1975
Black & White photo cards
of lots of monsters!
$15-20

SECRECY
Universal Games 1965
Spy game
$15-20

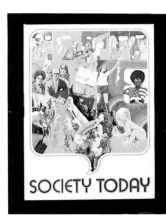

SOCIETY TODAY
Dynamic Design Ind 1971
Today's Issues
$5-7

THE FAMILY GAME
Dynamic Design Ind 1971
Working toward a well-adjusted
Nuclear Family
$5

WOMAN & MAN
Psychology Today 1971
"The Classic Confrontation"
$10-15
From the collection of Jeffrey Lowe.

BLACKS & WHITES
Psychology Today 1970
A look at the differences
between the Races
$15-20
From the collection of Jeffrey Lowe.

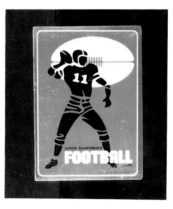

THE CITIES GAME
Psychology Today 1970
Urban Blight
$10-15
From the collection of Jeffrey Lowe.

BEAT DETROIT
Dynamic Games 1972
Planned obsolescence
$7-9

JR QUARTERBACK FOOTBALL GAME
BuiltRite 1960's
Miniature Bookshelf game
$8-10

4 QUARTER BASKETBALL GAME
BuiltRite 1960's
Miniature Bookshelf game
The series included Golf, Baseball,
Rummy, Hearts, Old Maid, Honeybears
and something called Bouquet
$8-10

CHUG-A-LUG
Dynamic Games 1969
"The Drinking Party Game"
Probably not M.A.D.D. approved
$7

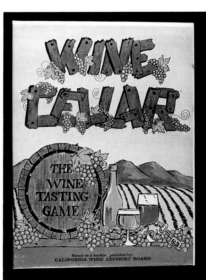

WINE CELLAR
Marina Enterprises 1971
Wine tasting game
(You provide the wine)
Comes with neat booklet
on varieties of wine, history, etc
$8-10

FOTO-ELECTRIC FOOTBALL
Cadaco 1965
"National! Pro Football
Hall of Fame Game"
$10-15

FOTO-ELECTRIC FOOTBALL
Cadaco-Ellis 1941
Wooden Box Version
$25-30

FOTO-ELECTRIC FOOTBALL
Cadaco-Ellis 1956
$10-12

FOTO-ELECTRIC FOOTBALL
Cadaco 1971
"Professional Football
Hall of Fame Game"
$8

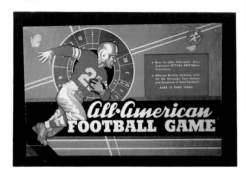

ALL-AMERICAN FOOTBALL GAME
Cadaco 1969
$8

ALL-AMERICAN FOOTBALL GAME
Cadaco 1960
$10

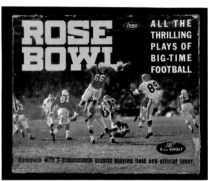

VARSITY
Cadaco-Ellis 1945
"The Scientific Football Game"
$10-15

COLLEGE FOOTBALL
Milton Bradley 1930's
$20-25

ROSE BOWL
E.S. Lowe 1966
$15

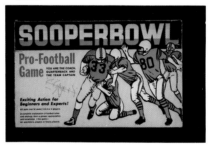

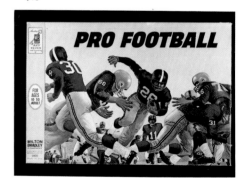

SAMSONITE PRO FOOTBALL GAME
Samsonite 1969
$10-15
From the collection of Jeffrey Lowe.

SOOPERBOWL PRO-FOOTBALL GAME
Sportswise Inc 1967
$8-10

PRO FOOTBALL
Milton Bradley 1964
$12-15

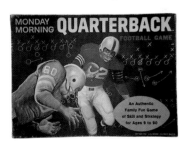

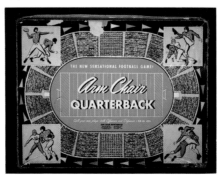

MONDAY MORNING QUARTERBACK FOOTBALL GAME
A.B. Zbinden 1963
$10-15
From the collection of Jeffrey Lowe.

ARM CHAIR QUARTERBACK
Novelty Mfg Co 1955
$15-18

QUARTERBACK
Transogram 1970
"Computerized Action Game"
$15-20
From the collection of Jeffrey Lowe.

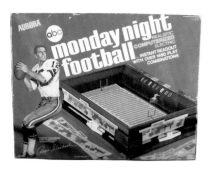

ABC MONDAY NIGHT FOOTBALL
AURORA 1972
Large plastic game
Endorsed by Roger Staubach
$15-20

SEE-ACTION FOOTBALL GAME
Kenner 1974
Give-A-Show technology
O.J. Simpson endorsed
$35-45
From the collection of Jeffrey Lowe.

TALKING FOOTBALL
Mattel 1971
Very large game uses small
records to describe action
There was also a TALKING MONDAY
NIGHT FOOTBALL GAME
$20-25

ALL-PRO FOOTBALL
Ideal 1967
"Official NFL Game"
$15-20

PRO DRAFT
Parker Brothers 1974
50 1974 Topps Trading Card
included
$25-30

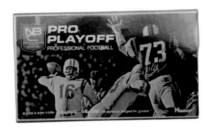

NBC PRO PLAYOFF
Hasbro 1969
NBC Sports in Action series
$10-12
From the collection of Jeffrey Lowe.

NBC GAME OF THE WEEK
Hasbro 1969
Sports in Action Baseball
$12-15
From the collection of Jeffrey Lowe.

ALL-STAR BASEBALL GAME
Cadaco 1960
$10

**ETHAN ALLEN'S MANAGER'S
SUPPLEMENT TO ALL-STAR BASEBALL**
Cadaco-Ellis 1957
Supplement supplies additional
stats for the game-Rare
$25-35
From the collection of Jeffrey Lowe.

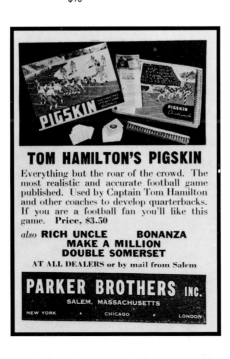

TOM HAMILTON'S PIGSKIN
Everything but the roar of the crowd. The
most realistic and accurate football game
published. Used by Captain Tom Hamilton
and other coaches to develop quarterbacks.
If you are a football fan you'll like this
game. Price, $3.50

also **RICH UNCLE   BONANZA
MAKE A MILLION
DOUBLE SOMERSET**
AT ALL DEALERS or by mail from Salem

PARKER BROTHERS INC.

SALEM, MASSACHUSETTS

NEW YORK   CHICAGO   LONDON

ALL-STAR BASEBALL GAME
Cadaco 1962
New Edition
$8-10

HOME TEAM BASEBALL
Selchow & Righter 1964
$5-8

33

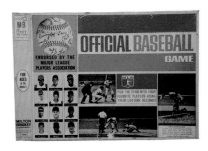

OFFICIAL BASEBALL GAME
Milton Bradley 1969
Includes trading cards
$150-250
From the collection of Jeffrey Lowe.

OFFICIAL BASEBALL CARD GAME
Milton Bradley 1970
Endorsed by the MLB Players
$65-100
From the collection of Jeffrey Lowe.

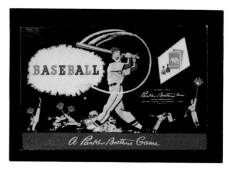

BASEBALL
Parker Brothers 1959
An earlier version exists
$20

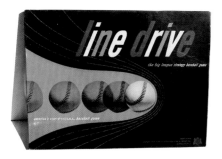

LINE DRIVE
Lord & Freber 1953
"The Big League Strategy
Baseball Game"
$20-25
From the collection of Jeffrey Lowe.

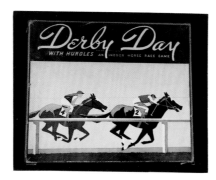

DERBY DAY WITH HURDLES
Parker Brothers 1930
Large indoor horse race game
Wooden horses
$25-35

DERBY DAY
Parker Brothers 1940's
$20-24
From the collection of Jeffrey Lowe.

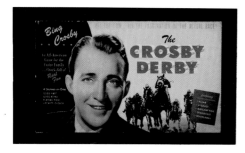

THE CROSBY DERBY
H. Fishlove & Co 1947
$30-50

HIALEAH HORSE RACING GAME
Milton Bradley 1940's
$20-25
From the collection of Jeffrey Lowe.

MAGIC-RACE
Habob 1940's
Believe it or not, you held
a lit cigarette to a chemically
treated sheet to
"Watch' Em Run!"
$20

NBC THE HOME STRETCH
Hasbro 1970
NBC Sports in Action
Thoroughbred Horse Racing
$10

SWEEPS
All-Fair 1940's
"The Popular 'Money' Game"
$20-25
From the collection of Jeffrey Lowe.

WIN, PLACE & SHOW
3M 1966
Horse Racing
$15-20

THE LONG GREEN
Milton Bradley 1936
"A Big Money Game of Chance"
Horse Racing
$15-20

THE CROSBY DERBY
H. Fishlove & Co 1947
Bing Crosby Horse Racing Game-Absolutely stunning
Graphics, with metal horses, win, place
and show stubs, and lots of money

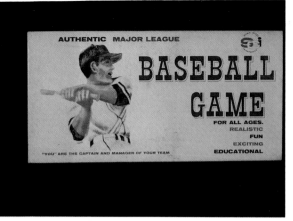

AUTHENTIC MAJOR LEAGUE BASEBALL GAME
Sports Games Inc 1962
$5-8

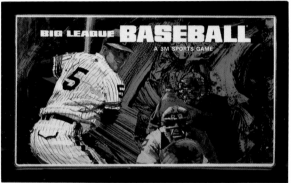

BIG LEAGUE BASEBALL
3M 1966
$12-15

MEL ALLEN'S BASEBALL GAME
Radio Corp of America 1959
A 33 1/3 record- "Mel Calls the
Plays, You Play the Game"
$10

BLUE LINE HOCKEY
3M 1970
$12-15
From the collection of Jeffrey Lowe.

REGATTA
3M 1967
Boating
$10-12

YACHT RACE
Parker Brothers 1961
Large elaborate game
Big metal boats
$25-30

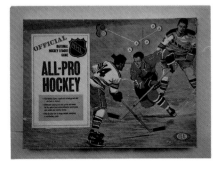

ALL-PRO HOCKEY
Ideal 1969
"Official NHL Game"
$10-15
From the collection of Jeffrey Lowe.

VOLLEY
Milton Bradley 1976
Volley ball
$10

QUICKFLIP VOLLEYBALL GAME
Ideal 1973
$12-15

THE SHUFFLE KING
Marx 1960's
Shuffle Board
$20-22

CHAMPION 6 IN 1 SPORTS COMBO
Transogram 1959
6 sports in handy carrying case
$15-20

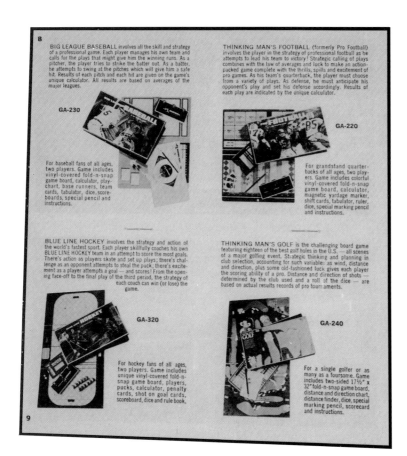

BIG LEAGUE BASEBALL involves all the skill and strategy of a professional game. Each player manages his own team and calls for the plays that might give him the winning runs. As a pitcher, the player tries to strike the batter out. As a batter, he attempts to swing at the pitches which will give him a safe hit. Results of each pitch and each hit are given on the game's unique calculator. All results are based on averages of the major leagues.

THINKING MAN'S FOOTBALL (formerly Pro Football) involves the player in the strategy of professional football as he attempts to lead his team to victory! Strategic calling of plays combines with the law of averages and luck to make an action-packed game complete with the thrills, spills and excitement of pro games. As his team's quarterback, the player must choose from a variety of plays. As defense, he must anticipate his opponent's play and set his defense accordingly. Results of each play are indicated by the unique calculator.

GA-230

For baseball fans of all ages, two players. Game includes vinyl-covered fold-n-snap game board, calculator, play-chart, base runners, team cards, tabulator, dice, score-boards, special pencil and instructions.

GA-220

For grandstand quarter-backs of all ages, two players. Game includes colorful vinyl-covered fold-n-snap game board, calculator, magnetic yardage marker, shift cards, tabulator, ruler, dice, special marking pencil and instructions.

BLUE LINE HOCKEY involves the strategy and action of the world's fastest sport. Each player skillfully coaches his own BLUE LINE HOCKEY team in an attempt to score the most goals. There's action as players skate and set up plays; there's challenge as an opponent attempts to steal the puck; there's excitement as a player attempts a goal — and scores! From the opening face-off to the final play of the third period, the strategy of each coach can win (or lose) the game.

THINKING MAN'S GOLF is the challenging board game featuring eighteen of the best golf holes in the U.S. — all scenes of a major golfing event. Strategic thinking and planning in club selection, accounting for such variables as wind, distance and direction, plus some old-fashioned luck gives each player the scoring ability of a pro. Distance and direction of shots — determined by the club used and a roll of the dice — are based on actual results records of pro tournaments.

GA-320

For hockey fans of all ages, two players. Game includes unique vinyl-covered fold-n-snap game board, players, pucks, calculator, penalty cards, shot on goal cards, scoreboard, dice and rule book.

GA-240

For a single golfer or as many as a foursome. Game includes two-sided 17½" x 32" fold-n-snap game board, distance and direction chart, distance finder, dice, special marking pencil, scorecard and instructions.

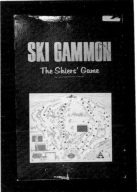

SKI GAMMON
American Publishing Corp 1962
"The Skiers' Game"
$5-7

TRACK MEET
Sports Illustrated 1972
$10

BRUCE JENNER DECATHALON GAME
Parker Brothers 1979
"Compete in 10 Exciting Events"
$12-15
From the collection of Jeffrey Lowe.

BAS-KET
Cadaco 1969
"Real Basketball in Miniature"
$10

36

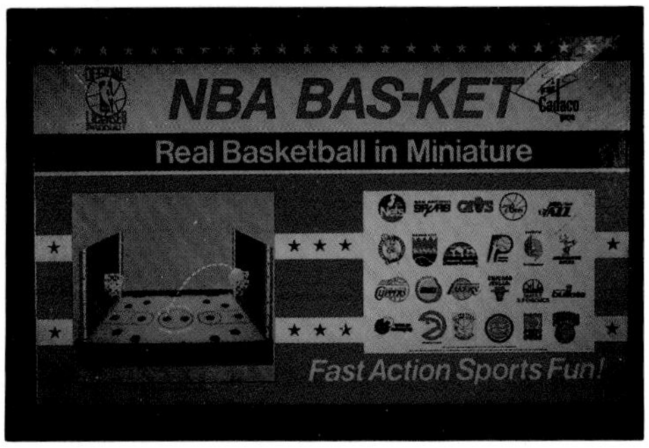

NBA BAS-KET
Cadaco 1983
$6-8

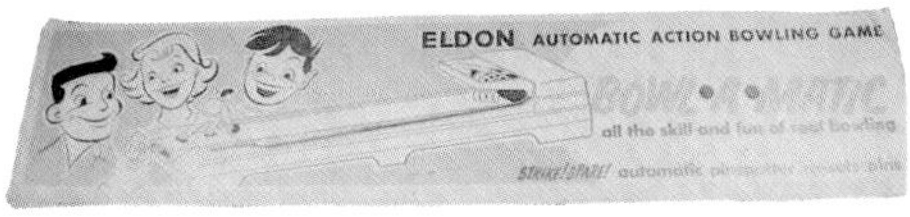

BOWL-A-MATIC
Eldon 1962
Huge all-plastic bowling toy
Automatically re-sets pins
$55-75

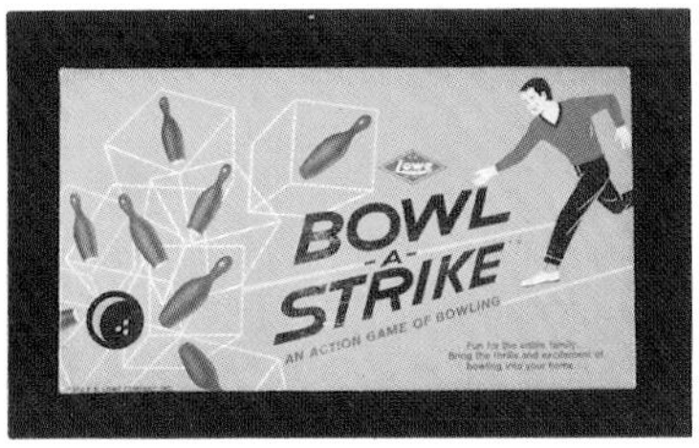

BOWL-A-STRIKE
E.S. Lowe 1962
Dice game
$5-7

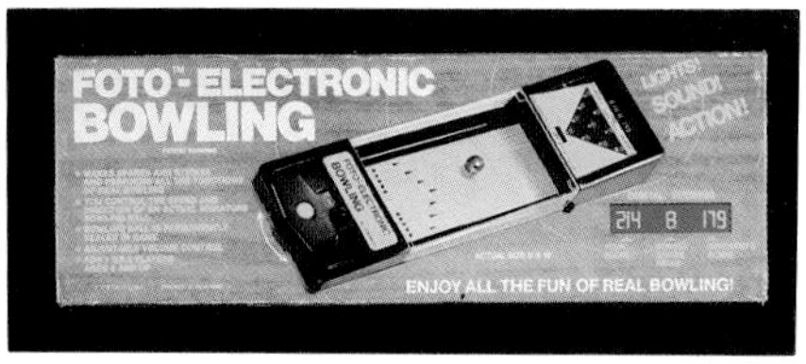

FOTO-ELECTRONIC BOWLING
Cadaco 1978
Early electronic game
Actually quite fun
$10-12

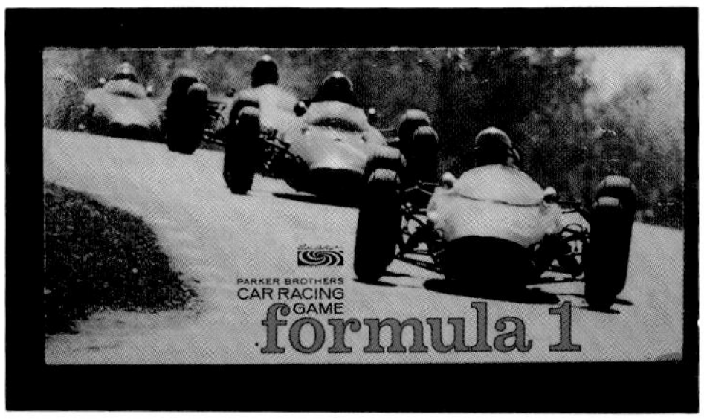

FORMULA 1
Parker Brothers 1964
$12-18

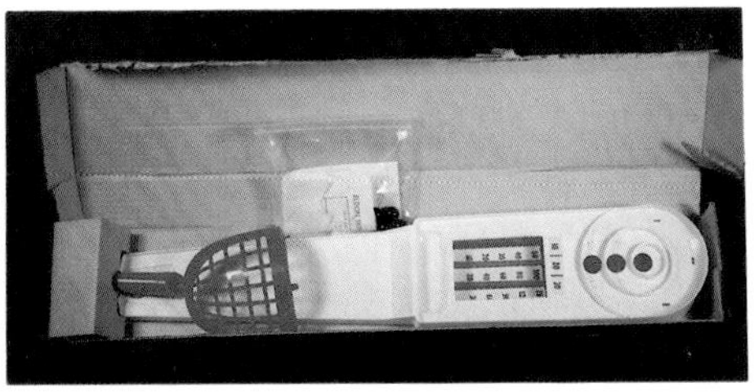

SKEE-BALL
Eldon 1965
Mail Order plastic set
$25

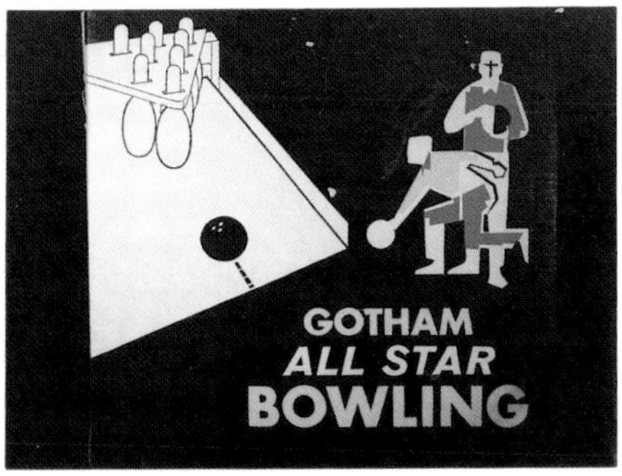

ALL STAR BOWLING
Gotham 1960's
Metal bowling game
$15-20

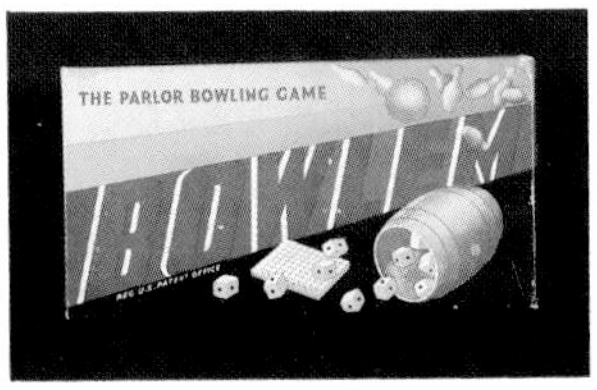

BOWL EM
Parker Brothers 1950's
Dice game-"The Parlor Bowling Game"
$7-10

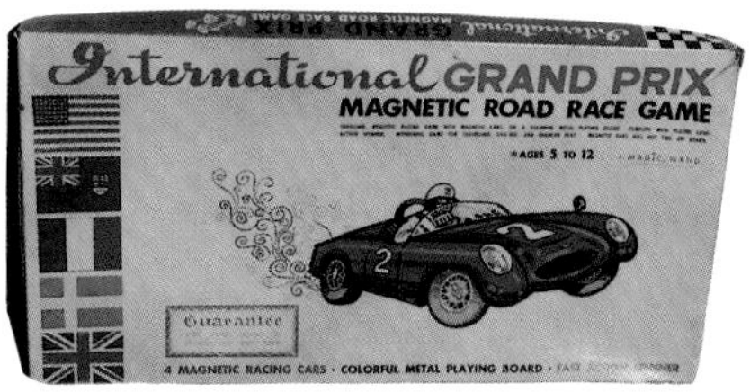

INTERNATIONAL GRAND PRIX
Magic Wand 1964
Magnetic Road Race Game
Same as COMBAT TANK
$15-20
From the collection of Jeffrey Lowe.

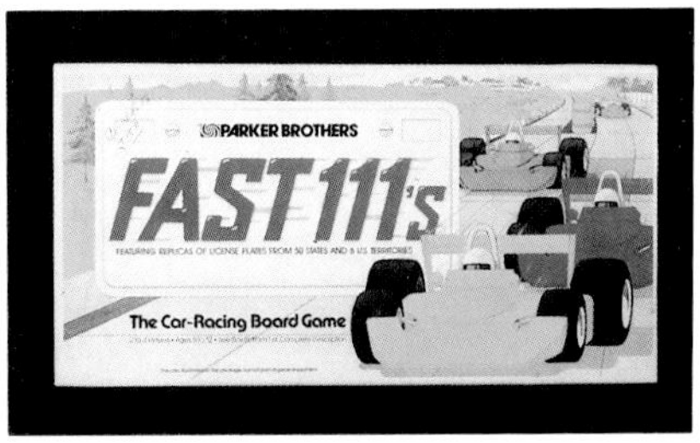

FAST 111'S
Parker Brothers 1981
Car racing game
$5

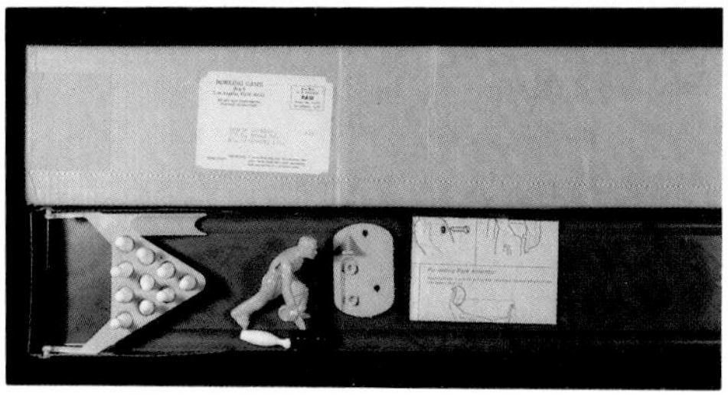

BOWLING GAME
Eldon 1960's
Mail Order plastic game
(Miniature version of BOWL-A-MATIC)
$20-24

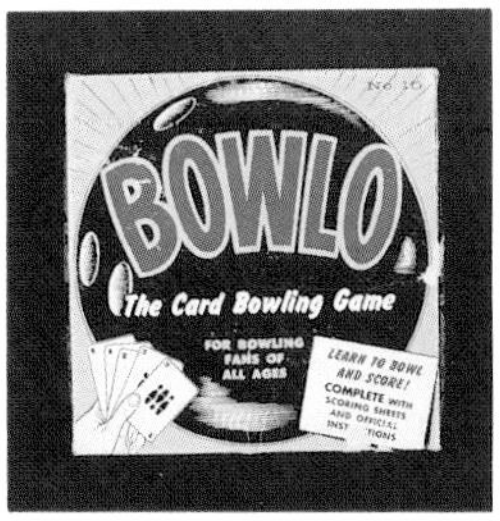

BOWLO
Feature Games 1957
$5-10

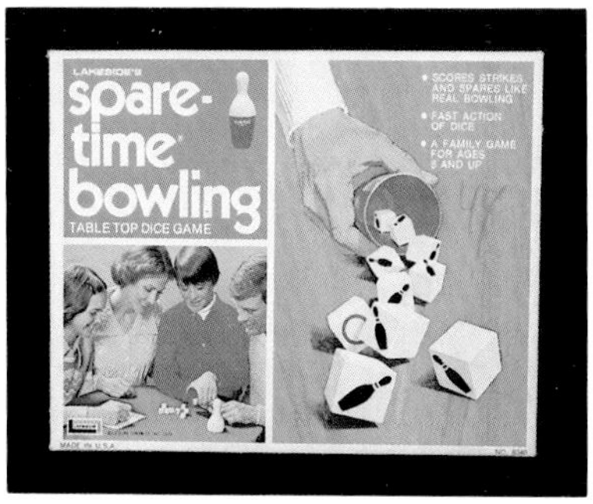

SPARE-TIME BOWLING
Lakeside 1974
Dice game
$5-8

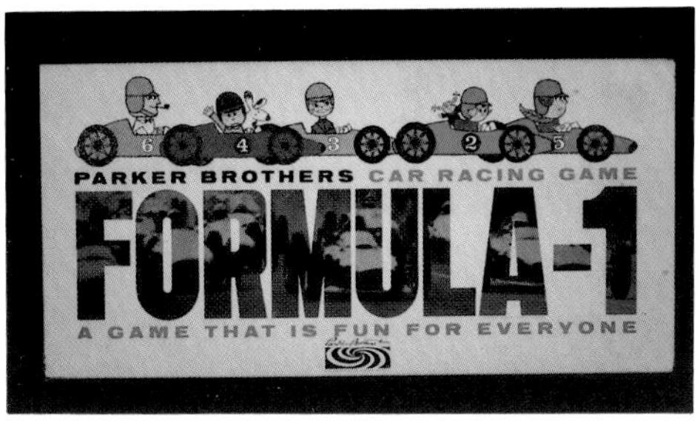

FORMULA-1
Parker Brothers 1963
Car racing game
$15-20

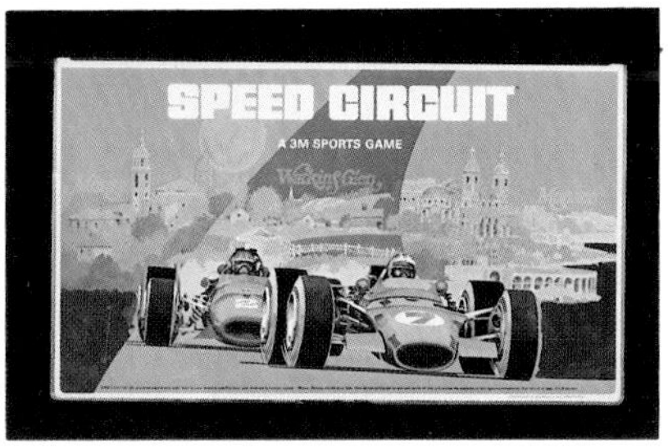

SPEED CIRCUIT
3M 1971
Car racing game
$10-15

RACE-O- RAMA GAME CHEST
BuiltRite 1960's
"4 Exciting Race Games"
$10-12

HUGGIN' THE RAIL
Selchow & Righter 1948
"Realistic Auto Race Game"
$20-25

DRAG STRIP!
Milton Bradley 1965
Skill & Action toy
$12-15

SPRINT
Mattel 1965
"Hot New Drag Race Game"
Very large, plastic
$25-30
From the Daniel Barr Collection.

DOG RACE
Transogram 1938
$15-20
From the collection of Jeffrey Lowe.

JIG CHASE
Game Makers 1940's
Dog Race game
Each player gets a jig saw puzzle
to put together as fast as they can
$15

JIG RACE
Game Makers 1940's
Same thing, only with
Horses- One more in this
series call JIG JUMP
From the collection of Jeffrey Lowe.
$10-15

THE HORSE RACING GAME
Milton Bradley 1936
$20-25
From the collection of Jeffrey Lowe.

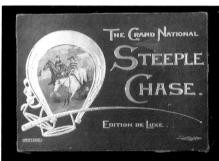

ACROSS THE BOARD HORSE RACING GAME
MPH 1975
"As Advertised in Readers' Digest"
$10-12
From the collection of Jeffrey Lowe.

GRAND NATIONAL
Whitman 1937
Horse racing game
$20-22
From the collection of Jeffrey Lowe.

SWEEPSTAKES
WM 1970's
"Electromatic Horse Race Game"
Very large game
$25-30

TOTOPOLY
Waddington 1949
"The Great Race Game"
$20-25
From the collection of Jeffrey Lowe.

THE GRAND NATIONAL STEEPLE CHASE
Spears Games 1920's
Edition De Luxe-Horse racing
$20-25

"THEY'RE OFF" HORSE RACE GAME
Parker Brothers 1950's
$25-30

THE AMERICAN DERBY
Cadaco-Ellis 1945
"Authorized by the Washington
Park Jockey Club"
$20-25
From the collection of Jeffrey Lowe.

BOWLO
Feature Games 1957
One of the few, if only, Card Bowling
games around- Everything you needed to get
a Strike, Spare, even a Gutter Ball!

KENTUCKY DERBY RACING GAME
Whitman 1938
Small game, metal horses
$10-12

DERBY DOWNS
Great Games 1973
Horse racing game
Comes with record
$10-12
From the collection of Jeffrey Lowe.

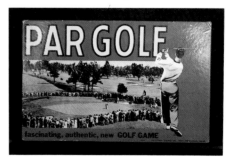

CAVALCADE
Selchow & Righter 1950's
Horse racing
$22-25
From the collection of Jeffrey Lowe.

THEY'RE AT THE POST
Maas Marketing 1976
Horse racing
Comes with records that
play races with different results
$10-15

FOTO-FINISH HORSE RACE
Pressman 1940
$15-17

PAR GOLF
National Games 1960's
$10-15

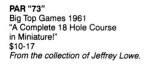

PAR "73"
Big Top Games 1961
"A Complete 18 Hole Course
in Miniature!"
$10-17
From the collection of Jeffrey Lowe.

PAR GOLF
W.M. Grimes 1959
Metal golf balls
$20-22

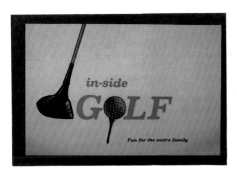

IN-SIDE GOLF
John M. Hall Enterprises 1967
$10-12

ACTION GOLF
Pressman 1960's
Metal game-Came with Club
and Ball- Other sports in this ACTION series
$20-25

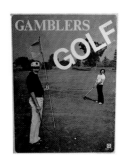

GAMBLERS GOLF
Gammon Games 1975
$10
From the collection of Jeffrey Lowe.

TEED OFF
Pacific Game Co 1972
Dice game
$5-7

GO FOR THE GREEN!
Time Inc 1973
$10-15
From the collection of Jeffrey Lowe.

THINKING MAN'S GOLF
3M 1966
$15-18

GARDNER'S CHAMPIONSHIP GOLF
Gardner Games 1960's
$20

TOURNAMENT GOLF
Rigely Banada 1969
"Green Valley Country Club"
$12-15

FORE
Artcraft Paper Products 1954
"Fun for Everyone in the Parlor
or Grill Room"
$15-20

LET'S PLAY GOLF
Burlu Enterprises 1968
"Waialae, Home of the Hawaiian Open"
There is a sought after Card Game
as well
$20-30

ULTIMATE GOLF
Ultimate Golf Inc 1985
"The Ultimate Game"
Beautiful, realistic game
$25-35

FAIRWAY GOLF
Trio Games Co 1954
Endorsed by Billy Maxwell
Fun game
$22-25

ARNOLD PALMER'S INSIDE GOLF
The David Bremson Co 1961
Huge game
"Fascinating as the Sport itself"
$25-35

MULLIGANS
San Fernando Valley Game Co 1947
"Pinehurst Championship Edition"
Other Editions were made
$22-26

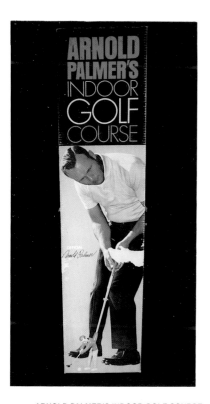

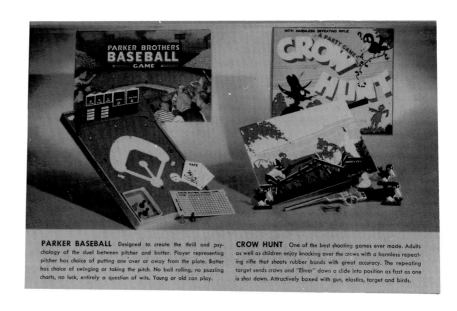

PARKER BASEBALL Designed to create the thrill and psychology of the duel between pitcher and batter. Player representing pitcher has choice of putting one over or away from the plate. Batter has choice of swinging or taking the pitch. No ball rolling, no puzzling charts, no luck, entirely a question of wits. Young or old can play.

CROW HUNT One of the best shooting games ever made. Adults as well as children enjoy knocking over the crows with a harmless repeating rifle that shoots rubber bands with great accuracy. The repeating target sends crows and "Elmer" down a slide into position as fast as one is shot down. Attractively boxed with gun, elastics, target and birds.

ARNOLD PALMER'S INDOOR GOLF COURSE
Marx 1968
Another large game
You manipulate a miniature golfer
via a Club-like handle
$35-55

The incredible incredible story behind MONOPOLY®, and how it became a legend in its own time.

© 1973 BY PARKER BROTHERS

Chapter 3

Monopoly

MONOPOLY, based on an older board game called THE LANDLORD'S GAME by Elizabeth Magie-Phillips, was developed and brought to Parker Brothers by Charles Darrow in 1934. Parker Brothers rejected the game, citing "52 fundamental errors" which included the potentially long length of the game (as opposed to ending at a specific time) and that the general public would not easily understand the real estate and rental concept. Charles Darrow believed otherwise and continued to market the game himself until Parker Brothers saw the error of their ways and bought the game outright in 1935, giving Darrow royalties on all games sold. Charles Darrow soon became a millionaire and retired at the age of forty-six.

To secure patents and copyrights, Parker Brothers also bought, developed and published FINANCE (created by Knapp Electric and influenced by THE LANDLORD'S GAME), FORTUNE, FINANCE AND FORTUNE, THE LANDLORD'S GAME (Magie-Phillips') and issued a patent to competitor Milton Bradley for a game called EASY MONEY. Transogram got into the act with a board game called BIG BUSINESS. All of these games were marketed around the same time and were similar to MONOPOLY, but they all owed a debt to the THE LANDLORD'S GAME. MONOPOLY has outlasted them all, and with good reason.

The lure of MONOPOLY is universal, as evidenced by the many different languages in which it is published. Almost everyone wants to be rich and powerful, and the game enables anyone to achieve this goal. Although the objective of driving your opponents into bankruptcy may seem a bit harsh at first glance, remember it's all part of the fun.

The docile clerk can become the merciless hotel financier, snatching bankrupt properties from howling foes; or trusting little Timmy becomes the savvy holdout, knowing you only need his READING RAILROAD to complete your takeover of the railways. Anyone anywhere can play, and everyone has their own strategy. Many people also have their own version of the rules which, although not appearing in the official transcripts, are nonetheless inviolable.

There were Popular Editions, Standard Editions, Library Editions, Gold Editions...even a De Luxe Edition that sold for $25.00 in the 1930s and included items like metal money and large tokens with a gold finish. A Stock Exchange addendum was offered in 1936 that converted the Free Parking space on the board into the "Stock Exchange." Early Community Chest cards read "We're off the Gold Standard - collect $50" and have long since changed. During the rationing of World War II, a cardboard insert was included that explained that cellophane would no longer be used to wrap the implements of the game. There have been wood pieces, composition pieces, metal pieces and in Charles Darrow's original game, no pieces. You were supposed to supply your own. There have been sets made out of chocolate and sets made out of gold. But perhaps no set is as precious as the family game that is handed down to you.

Strangely, other than the original Charles Darrow games or the Wanamaker Department Store sets or the inaugural 1935 Parker Brothers sets, there is little collector interest in old MONOPOLY games. This is probably because literally millions of sets were produced with very little variation. However, if you look closely, it is possible to see interesting changes that delineate one edition from another through the years. Additionally, in recent times, a host of different games have been spun off from the original MONOPOLY game, which continues to be enormously successful.

All in all, the fame of MONOPOLY has spread through out the world, sowing a little bit of capitalism and fantasy wherever it goes. No matter in what part of the world the game is played, everyone dreads picking up a card that reads "GO DIRECTLY TO JAIL. DO NOT PASS GO. DO NOT COLLECT $200". Rest assured, though, it could be worse. You might land on BOARDWALK...with a hotel on it!

Some of the 5000 MONOPOLY sets Darrow had printed and sold to Wanamakers Department Store in Philadelphia. The Parker Brothers 1936 STOCK EXCHANGE. Accessory can be seen in the background.

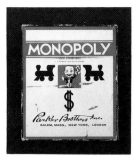

MONOPOLY
Parker Brothers 1936-1943
So many sets were made that it's difficult to tell them apart. Two patent numbers were printed until 1943, so this set could be from any year.
$10-15

A rare "Wartime Restrictions" cardboard cover replaced the cellophane coverage on this utensils box.

MONOPOLY
Parker Brothers 1935
The date 1935 and two patent numbers means its from 1935-Metal pieces.
$15-18

MONOPOLY
Parker Brothers 1943 and later
One patent number could mean the set is after 1943.
$8-10

MONOPOLY
Parker Brothers 1943 and later
Although this is a later game, early Boards tend to have no illustration on the Community Chest Space, the Community Chest and Chance cards have no illustration, Copyright Charles Darrow in the Jail space and their may be metal moving pieces.

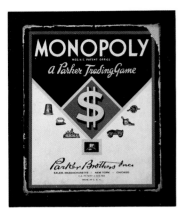

MONOPOLY
Parker Brothers 1930's
With metal pieces
$15-20

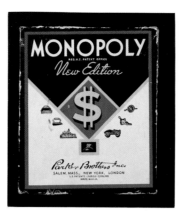

MONOPOLY
Parker Brothers 1936?
New Edition
$15-20

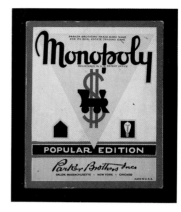

MONOPOLY
Parker Brothers 1950's
Popular Edition was one up
from the Standard Edition
Red Border
$8-10

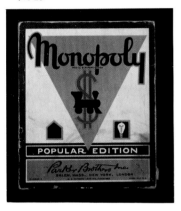

MONOPOLY
Parker Brothers 1930's
Popular Edition
Green border
$10-15

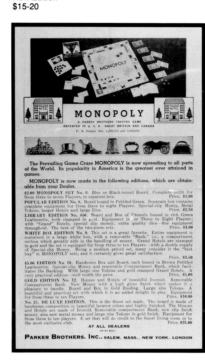

This ad shows all the Editions available in the late 1930's.
The White Box Edition (No. 9) was a favorite, but take a look
at the De Luxe Edition.

Community Chest and Chance
Cards from a transistion
period between no
illustration and The Rich
Uncle.

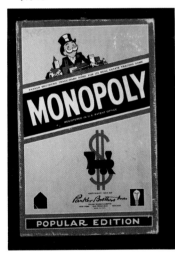

MONOPOLY
Parker Brothers 1954 and later
Rich Uncle Pennybags adorns this
later Popular Edition
Wooden pawns-Red border
$5-10

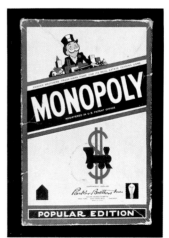

MONOPOLY
Parker Brothers 1954
Popular Edition
Green border
$5-10

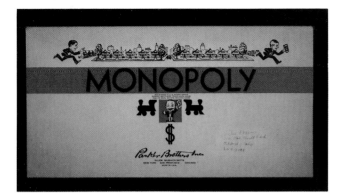

MONOPOLY
Parker Brothers 1950's
White Box Edition No. 9
with Grand Hotels
$10-20

MONOPOLY
Parker Brothers 1940's thru 1960's
The illustration of the playing
board on the cover separates this
common edition from others-
Plastic houses
$5- 7

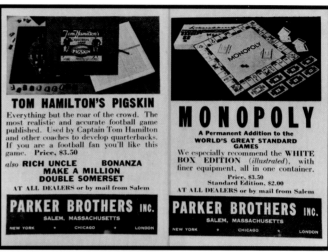

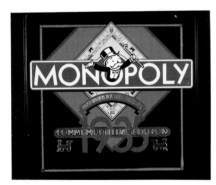

MONOPOLY
Parker Brothers 1985
Commemorative Edition
Metal box with Gold Tokens
and Grand Hotels celebrates
the 50th Anniversary (1935)
$15-20

MONOPOLY
Parker Brothers 1957
Unusual train cover
$12-15

MONOPOLY
Parker Brothers 1960's-1970's
Uncommon Deluxe Edition with
Styrofoam money holder
$10-12

MONOPOLY
Parker Brothers 1968
Common edition showing
the General Mills logo, a company
who acquired Parker Brothers in
the late 1960's.
$5-8
Courtesy of Grace Tanaka.

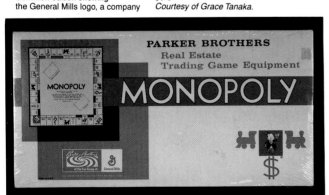

MONOPOLY
Parker Brothers 1978
Photo cover Deluxe Edition
It celebrates an anniversary
but I can't figure out which one
$8-10

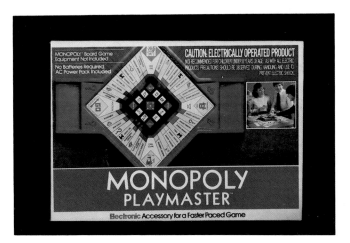

MONOPOLY PLAYMASTER
Parker Brothers 1982
When placed in the middle
of your set, it kept track of
all the moves.
$10-15

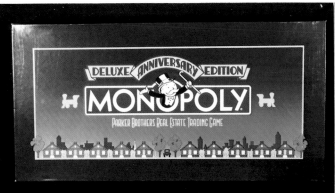

MONOPOLY
Parker Brothers 1985
Deluxe Anniversary Edition
with metal pieces and Grand
Hotels
$7-10

RICH UNCLE STOCK MARKET GAME
Parker Brothers 1959
MONOPOLY spin-off featuring a slightly
altered Rich Uncle Pennybags.

RICH UNCLE STOCK MARKET GAME
Parker Brothers 1959
$15-20

Ad for yet another version of RICH UNCLE

RICH UNCLE THE STOCK MARKET GAME
Parker Brothers 1955
$20-25

DIG
Parker Brothers 1950's
Rich Uncle Pennybags appeared
on the cover and cards of this
"Lively Action Game"
$5-10

DIG
Parker Brothers 1950's
"The Pick Does the Trick"
$5-7

DIG
Parker Brothers 1968
Rich Uncle is but a memory
$3-5

47

MONOPOLY
Waddington 1961
British Version
$5-10

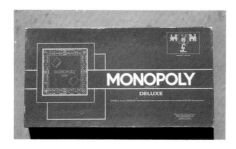

MONOPOLY
Waddington 1972
Deluxe British Edition
$10-15

MONOPOLY
Waddington 1971
British Edition
$5-7

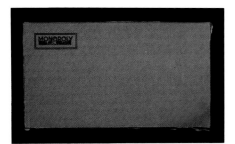

MONOPOLY
? 1930's
French Edition
Round playing tokens
$20-30

MONOPOLY
Parker Brothers 1985
French Edition
$10

MONOPOLY
Parker Brothers 1988
Russian Edition
"Special Limited Edition"
$10-15

MONOPOLY
Parker Brothers 1992
German Edition
$10-12

MONOPOLY
Parker Brothers 1978
Spanish Edition
$5-10

MONOPOLY
Parker Brothers 1988
Japanese Edition
Tomy-a division of Tonka?
$5- 7

MONOPOLY
Parker Brothers 1980's
Japanese Edition
I'm not sure what is being
explained in the directions, but
it sure looks weird
$10-15

The Franklin Mint continues to
manufacture a beautiful edition
in sterling silver and 24 karat gold

The California Lottery got in the
act with MONOPOLY SCRATCHERS...
"Inherit $10,000 from a Rich Uncle"

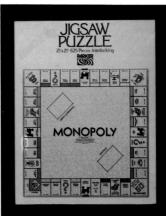

'84 L.A. GAMES MONOPOLY
A GK Games 1984
This game was sold during the
(you guessed it) 1984 Olympics
but pulled from the shelves as
an unauthorized knockoff, making
it a collectible
$20-25

Jigsaw puzzles were made as
well as clocks, watches, paperweights,
even a cooking apron.

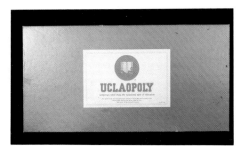

UCLAOPOLY
Late For The Sky Prd Co 1989
One of a myriad college or city
"Opolies" games
$10-12

ANTI-MONOPOLY
Ralph Anspach 1973
"The 'Bust-the-Trust!' Game"
Well-publicized Parker Brothers lawsuit forced
Anspach to yank this game and
bury remaining copies in a landfill.
Decision was later overturned and game
was allowed to be sold.
$15-20

ANTI
National Games 1977
"The Trust Buster's Game"
Same game as ANTI-MONOPOLY
but without the crucial word
"Monopoly" after court ruled
against him.
$20-24

MONOPOLY
Parker Brothers 1980's
Braille Edition
$25-35

ADVANCE TO BOARDWALK
Parker Brothers 1985
Spin-off of a space on the
MONOPOLY board
$5-8

FREE PARKING
Parker Brothers 1988
"Feed the Meter Game"
Card game
$3-5

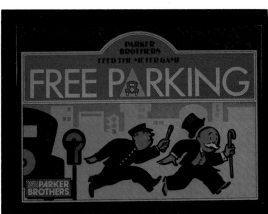

DON'T GO TO JAIL
Parker Brothers 1991
Dice game
$5-7

EXPRESS MONOPOLY CARD GAME
Parker Brothers 1993
Card game
$5

MONOPOLY JUNIOR
Parker Brothers 1990
Now the small fry can
play too!
$4-7

49

Chapter 4

General

General games could best be described as "everyday" games, and constitute everything that does not really pertain to a specific theme. Although a case could be made for dividing general games into sub-categories (i.e. "plastic games" or "marble games") it would be pointless to do so.

This section includes such classics as Milton Bradley's CHUTES AND LADDERS and Parker Brothers' SORRY. There are popular card and dice games here, such as Parker Brothers' PIT and E.S. Lowe's YAHTZEE, as well as many large plastic games by Ideal, like TIP-IT and KA-BOOM!

The illustrations on game boxes often succeed as art in their own right, as in Hasbro's MENTOR or Milton Bradley's INTRIGUE. Whatever artistic elements attracted our attention years ago, attract us still.

To many board game collectors, the playability of a game is not important. The subtle aesthetics of a game, coupled with the nostalgia factor inherent within the collector themselves, will generally be the dominant elements in the desirability of a game, and determine how much a collector will pay.

Here is a portion of the thousands of games that have been manufactured over the years...

GO TO THE HEAD OF THE CLASS
Milton Bradley 1955
Series 7
$7-9

GO TO THE HEAD OF THE CLASS
Milton Bradley 1967
Series 17
$3-5

CHUTES AND LADDERS
Milton Bradley 1943
Original Edition
$15-20

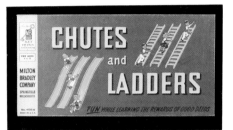

CHUTES AND LADDERS
Milton Bradley 1950's
$20-25

CHUTES AND LADDERS
Milton Bradley 1956
$10-15

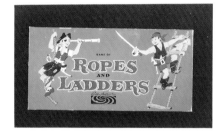

GAME OF ROPES AND LADDERS
Parker Brothers 1954
Parker's attempt to cash in on
CHUTES AND LADDERS
$10-15

CANDYLAND GAME
Milton Bradley 1962
Popular game of colors
$15-25

FOREST FRIENDS
Milton Bradley 1956
"A Cute Little Folks Animal Game"
$7-10

THE HAPPY LITTLE TRAIN GAME
Milton Bradley 1957
$10-12

CARDINO
Milton Bradley 1970
Tile Strategy game
$5-7

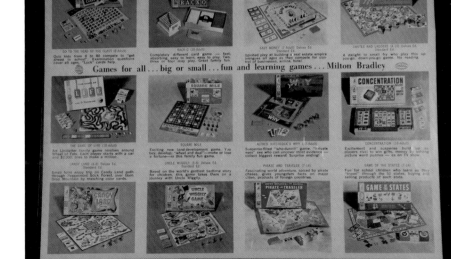

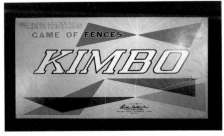

KIMBO
Parker Brothers 1960
"Game of Fences"
$10-20

QUICK SHOOT GAME
Ideal 1970
"Game of Rootin' Tootin' Marble
Shootin'!"
$10-13

THE GAME OF BLAST
Ideal 1973
Similar to BATTLE BOARD
$10

BEE BOPPER GAME
Ideal 1968
Catch flying "Bees"
$20

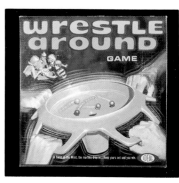

WRESTLE AROUND GAME
Ideal 1969
$10-15

BATTLING TOPS GAME
Ideal 1968
Spinning tops battle it out
$12-15

TORNADO BOWL GAME
Ideal 1971
Distant cousin of BATTLING TOPS
$10-12

TOSS ACROSS GAME
Ideal 1969
Tic Tac Toe with Bean Bags
Marvin Glass Design
$10-15

LUCKY STAR GUM BALL GAME
Ideal 1961
"You Pay, Play, Chew Away"
$25-30

THE GREAT ESCAPE
Ideal 1967
Players are handcuffed to the
board until they can get the
key that frees them
$25

POISON IVY GAME
Ideal 1969
Players pick leaves from a patch
and hope they don't get one with
"Poison Ivy"
$20-22

EGG RACE GAME
Ideal 1968
$15-20

COLD FEET
Ideal 1967
"The 'Squirt' Game"
$20-22
Courtesy of Rick Polizzi.

SLAP TRAP GAME
Ideal 1967
Marvin Glass Design
$20-25
From the collection of Jeffrey Lowe.

THE BIG SNEEZE GAME
Ideal 1968
$20-23

SWACK! GAME
Ideal 1968
$20-25

THE GAME OF TIGER ISLAND
Ideal 1966
Feed the Tiger marbles before
he smacks you with a club-
Marvin Glass design
$25-35

HANDS DOWN
Ideal 1964
"Featuring the Slam-O-Matic!"
$20

OH, NUTS! GAME
Ideal 1969
Try to find your color
marbles hidden within the nuts
$20-22

BUCK-A-ROO! GAME
Ideal 1970
Similar to THE LAST STRAW
$15-20

CHOP SUEY GAME
Ideal 1967
$15-20

TIP-IT
Ideal 1965
"The Wackiest Balancing Game Ever!"
$10-15

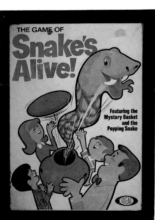

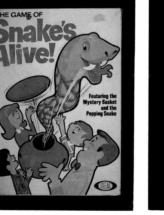

THE GAME OF HOOPLA
Ideal 1966
Skill game
Marvin Glass design
$20-25
From the collection of Jeffrey Lowe.

THE GAMES OF SNAKE'S ALIVE!
Ideal 1966
Poke the wrong part of the
basket and the snake pops out
$20-24

GRAND SLAM GAME
Ideal 1969
$15-20

HANG ON HARVEY! GAME
Ideal 1969
Remove pegs to make
"Harvey" scale down the wall
$15-20

KERPLUNK
Ideal 1967
$15-20

BLOWOUT GAME
Ideal 1978
Similar to KA-BOOM!
$10-12

POPPIN HOPPIES GAME
Ideal 1968
Catch spring loaded "Hoppies"
$20-25

53

PINHEAD
Remco 1959
Track game
$18-25

MELVIN THE MOON MAN
Remco 1960's
From a series of "Tumblebum"
Dice Games- They all had 4 large
moving pieces, a huge playing
mat "board" and a deck of cards
$25-45

BANG BOX GAME
Ideal 1969
$18-22

LOOK OUT BELOW GAME
Ideal 1968
Balancing game-
Marvin Glass design
$18-20

FLAP JACK
Remco 1960's
"The Flip-Flop Game"
$20-24

NOTCH
Remco 1960's
Uncommon
$35-45

SHMO
Remco 1959
"I'm a Shmo and that
ain't good"
$25-35

GIANT WHEEL COWBOYS 'N INDIANS
Remco 1958
"Giant Wheel" series included PICTURE BINGO
and THRILLS 'N SPILLS HORSE RACE
$35-45
From the collection of Jeffrey Lowe.

JUNGLE SKITTLES
American Toy Works 1950's
Knock down pins
$25-35

HOT POTATO
Remco 1960's
Don't be left holding
the potato when the timer
runs out
$20-25

HATS OFF BOWLING GAME
Transogram 1944
Knock the hats off the
clowns
$10-15

SKITTLE-BOWL
Aurora 1969
Classic bowling game
$15-25

STAMPIN'
Rainy Day Design 1989
A Philatelist's dream
$7-10

HATS' OFF
Kohner 1967
Flip your color "Hats" into your color section
$7-15

BASH!
Milton Bradley 1965
$12-18

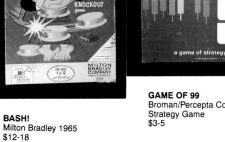

GAME OF 99
Broman/Percepta Corp 1963
Strategy Game
$3-5

SWACK! GAME
Ideal 1968
The object was to remove little pieces
of plastic cheese without causing the
trap to go Swack!- The cover illustration
Mousetrap looked like it could take your arm off.

POP YER TOP!
Milton Bradley 1968
Hop the "Bird" without popping
his top
$20-24

SHENANIGANS CARNIVAL OF FUN GAME
Milton Bradley 1964
From the Game Show, there is a
cover version featuring Stubby Kaye
$15-20

KOOKY CARNIVAL GAME
Milton Bradley 1969
2 cover versions
$12-17

BUG-A-BOO GAME
Whitman 1968
Tin wind-up "bugs" provided the
action
$10-13

SWAP
Ideal 1965
Object being to "Out-Swap
Everyone"-Marvin Glass design
$15-20

FEELEY MEELEY
Milton Bradley 1967
"The Game That Gives You a
Funny Feeling!"-Marvin Glass design
$20-25

DYNAMITE SHACK GAME
Milton Bradley 1968
"Exciting But Perfectly Safe"-
Marvin Glass design
$20-25
Courtesy of Rick Polizzi.

FRANTIC FROGS
Milton Bradley 1965
Tin wind-up "Frogs" were guided
to your corner of the board
$25-30

55

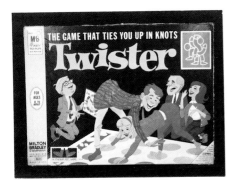

TWISTER
Milton Bradley 1966
Famous game that "Ties You Up
in Knots"
$10-15

GRAB A LOOP
Milton Bradley 1968
Kind of like Tag Football
$20-22

SWIVEL
Milton Bradley 1972
Dig them crazy threads!
$20

SLAP STICK
Milton Bradley 1966
$20-23

BUCKET OF FUN
Milton Bradley 1968
Take my word for it, don't
stick your face in the bucket
when it's ready to pop...
$20-27

LIMBO LEGS
Milton Bradley 1969
"Jump Over the Limbo Stick"-
Marvin Glass design
15-20

HIGH GEAR GAME
Mattel 1962
"The 'Mechanical Maneuver' Game"
$20-25

FEED THE ELEPHANT!
Cadaco-Ellis 1952
Catapult "Peanuts" into the Elephant's mouth
$10-15

PITCHIN' PAL
Cadaco-Ellis 1953
$10-15
From the collection of Jeffrey Lowe.

SAD SAM THE TARGET-BALL MAN
Whitman 1966
Pitch balls into holes on Sad Sam's face.
$5-10

MASTERPIECE
Parker Brothers 1970
"The Art Auction Game"
Marvin Glass design
$5-12

THE INVENTORS
Parker Brothers 1974
Marvin Glass design
$7-10

KOMMISSAR
Selchow & Righter 1966
"The People's Game"
$15-20

WHO?
Parker Brothers 1951
$20-30
From the collection of Jeffrey Lowe.

CAREERS
Parker Brothers 1958
"Game of Optional Goals"
$10-15

GURU
E.S. Lowe 1969
"The Think Game for Swingers
of All Ages"
$10-15
From the collection of Jeffrey Lowe.

SIMON SAYS
Warren 1970's
Simplistic board/cardgame
$3-5

MERRY-GO-ROUND GAME
Whitman 1965
3-D "hill" turns, diverting
playing piece
$10-12

WHODUNIT?
Cadaco-Ellis 1959
CLUE-like game
$20-25
From the collection of Jeffrey Lowe.

CAREERS
Parker Brothers 1965
$7

THE GAME OF LOVE
Hasbro 1960's
From the "Loveable Game" series
$20-23
Courtesy of Rick Polizzi.

WHOSIT?
Parker Brothers 1976
Guess the identities
$7-10

ENGINEER
Selchow & Righter 1957
Railroad-Track game
$10-15

SPIN THE BOTTLE GAME
Hasbro 1968
You perform odd stunts when
the bottle points your way
$17-20

57

FASCINATION
Remco 1961
"The Electric Maze Game"
$20-25

FASCINATION
Remco 1961
$20-25

FASCINATION
Remco 1968
$15

FASCINATION POOL
Remco 1962
$10-15

FASCINATION CHECKERS
Remco 1960's
$15-20

HIPPOPOTAMUS
Remco 1961
Similar to FASCINATION
$20-25

VOICE OF THE MUMMY
Milton Bradley 1971
$25-40

SEANCE
Milton Bradley 1972
Sequel to VOICE OF THE MUMMY
$25-35

BEHIND THE "8" BALL GAME
Selchow & Righter 1969
The fortune-telling "8" ball
adapted to a card game
$10-15

STUMP CARD GAME
Milton Bradley 1968
$5-7

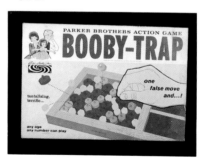

BOOBY-TRAP
Parker Brothers 1965
"One False Move and..." Bang!
little round wood things everywhere
$10-15

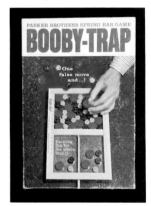

BOOBY-TRAP
Parker Brothers 1960's
$10-13

THE GAME OF ASSEMBLY LINE
Selchow & Righter 1950's
"Assemble Cars Like the Motor Czars"
Tons of plastic pieces
$20-25

THE GAME OF ASSEMBLY LINE
Selchow & Righter 1960's
$15-17

CARS N' TRUCKS BUILD-A-GAME
Ideal 1961
Assemble cars and trucks
$25-35
From the collection of Jeffrey Lowe.

CRISS CROSS
Ideal 1971
$10-12

RATTLE BATTLE
Parker Brothers 1970
"Quick Draw Marble Game"
$5-10

HURRY UP
Parker Brothers 1971
Marble race game
$5-7

FAST EDDIE GAME
Mattel 1970
Marbles game
$5-7

BOUNDARY
Mattel 1970
Strategy games with strings
$5-8
From the collection of Jeffrey Lowe.

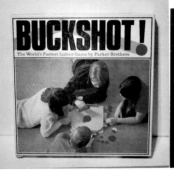

MINDMAZE
Parker Brothers 1970
Marvin Glass design
$10

BUCKSHOT!
Parker Brothers 1970
"World's Fastest Indoor Game"
$7-10
From the collection of Jeffrey Lowe.

AUCTIONEER
Ideal 1972
Timer gives you limited
time to bid on objects before
plastic gavel bangs down
$15-20

GOING! GOING! GONE!
Milton Bradley 1975
"The Flea Market Auction Game"
$10-12

DEAD STOP! GAME
Milton Bradley 1979
Use your "Deductive Powers"
$5-7

TROUBLE
Kohner 1965
Featuring the "Pop-O-Matic"
$5-7

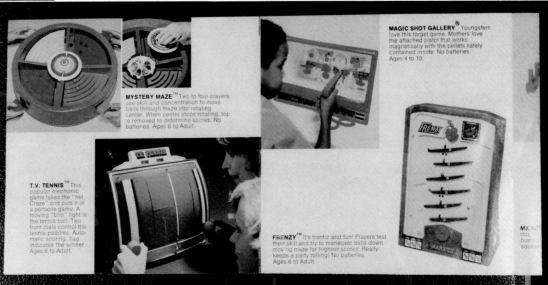

PROBE
Parker Brothers 1964
Word game
$4-6

PROBE
Parker Brothers 1974
$3-5

4 CYTE
McGraw Hill Book Co 1963
Word game-Original Edition
$7-9

4 CYTE
Milton Bradley 1967
Twin Set Table Model
$10-12

ACROSS THE CONTINENT
Parker Brothers 1952
"The United States Game"
Metal pieces
$20-25

ACROSS THE CONTINENT
Parker Brothers 1960
$15-20
From the collection of Jeffrey Lowe.

WIDE WORLD TRAVEL GAME
Parker Brothers 1957
Metal jet playing pieces
$20-25

WIDE WORLD
Parker Brothers 1962
$20
From the collection of Jeffrey Lowe.

CARGOES
Selchow & Righter 1930's
(board not shown) Trade game
$20-25

CARGOES
Selchow & Righter 1950's
William Longyear illustration
$20

CARGOES
Selchow & Righter 1958
$10-13

TO THE SALES CLERK

Know Your Merchandise and Increase Your Sales

Here are the outstanding features of CARGOES

1. A game suitable for any boy or girl over 8 years.

2. An educational travel Game, for 2, 3 or 4 players.

3. Players travel to Seaports all over the world, picking up fascinating Cargoes and unloading merchandise at each port.

4. Teaches geography and acquaints the players with the proper exports and imports for each part of the World.

5. Players encounter all the thrills experienced by real Sea Captains.

6. The illustrated Map and Cargoes are of endless interest.

The first player then starts his voyag

SUPER SPY
Milton Bradley 1971
"The Electric Alarm Game"
Players tried to gather information
while avoiding "alarmed" sections
of the floor.

UNDERCOVER
Cadaco-Ellis 1960
Game made use of special
"Infra-Scope Goggles"
$25-30
From the collection of Jeffrey Lowe.

CONSPIRACY
Milton Bradley 1982
"All the Excitement of
International Espionage!"
$5-7

ENEMY AGENT
Milton Bradley 1976
with unique "Passport Scanner"
$8-10

AVANTE
Franes 1967
Strategy game
$3-5

HARPOON
Gabriel 1955
Miniature Whales
$25-30
From the collection of Jeffrey Lowe.

SUPER SPY
Milton Bradley 1971
$15-20

SPECIAL DETECTIVE/SPEEDWAY
Saalfield 1959
Two games in one!
$15-20
From the collection of Jeffrey Lowe.

SPECIAL AGENT
Parker Brothers 1966
$10-12
From the collection of Jeffrey Lowe.

A GAME ABOUT THE UNITED NATIONS
Payton Products 1961
$20-25
From the collection of Jeffrey Lowe.

INTERNATIONAL GAME OF SPY
All-Fair 1940's
$25-35
From the collection of Jeffrey Lowe.

MANIAC ELECTRONIC GAME
Ideal 1979
SIMON SAYS style game
$10

PLUS ONE
Milton Bradley 1980
Electronic maze-like game
$10

THE WELFARE GAME & A MODEST SOLUTION
St. Croix, Inc 1971
Shows how to "Stop Spiraling Welfare Costs"
$10-14

LASER ATTACK GAME
Milton Bradley 1978
Don't get hit by the
"Dreaded Enemy Laser"
$10-13

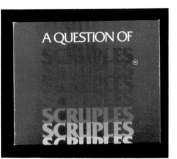

MELTDOWN
Storeplay Inc 1980's
"The Nuclear Energy Conflict Game"
$5-8

I.D.
Milton Bradley 1988
"The Identity Game"
$5-7

A QUESTION OF SCRUPLES
High Game Enterprises 1984
Original Edition
$10

ENERGY QUEST
Weldon Productions 1977
MONOPOLY like game involving
search for alternate fuel
$8-10

SOLARQUEST
Golden 1986
MONOPOLY in outer space
$7-10

GOOSES WILD
Co-5 Company 1966
Dice game
$5-7

THE GAME OF TRIPOLEY
Cadaco-Ellis 1936
You supplied the cards
$5-7

THE GAME OF TRIPOLEY
Cadaco-Ellis 1936
(board opened)

THE GAME OF TRIPOLEY
Cadaco-Ellis 1942
Service Edition
$7-9

TRIPOLEY
Cadaco 1969
Deluxe Layout
$4

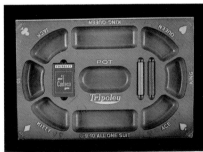

TRIPOLEY
Cadaco 1968
$7-9

TRIPOLEY
Cadaco 1965
De luxe Edition
$5-6

SPLURGE
Createk 1968
Gambling game
$10

VEGAS
Milton Bradley 1973
Skill/Luck game
$7-9

GAMBLER
Parker Brothers 1977
A different way to gamble
on every space
$5-7

63

THE ORIGINAL AGGRAVATION GAME
CO-5 Company 1962
Marble and dice game
$5-7

AGGRAVATION
CO-5 Company 1960's
Deluxe Party Edition
$3-5

AGGRAVATION
Lakeside 1970
Standard Edition
$3-5

SPLIT-LEVEL AGGRAVATION
Lakeside 1971
$5-7

HI-HO! CHERRY-O
Whitman 1960
Plastic cherry-picking game
$10

HI-HO SANTA CLAUS GAME
Whitman 1962
Plastic ornaments-
Florence Sarah Winship cover
$1 5- 2 0

THE GAME SCOOP!
Parker Brothers 1956
"Publish Your Own Newspaper"
$25-35
From the collection of Jeffrey Lowe.

SCOOP
Waddington 1955
British version
$25-30

STAR REPORTER
Parker Brothers 1960
Same game as BOAKE CARTER'S
STAR REPORTER GAME
$15-20

INTRIGUE
Milton Bradley 1950
$25-35

INTRIGUE
Milton Bradley 1955
$20-25

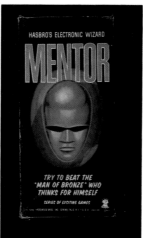

PERFECTION
Lakeside 1973
Fit the pieces into place before
the timer pops them out
$5-7

DEDUCTION
Ideal 1976
"The Game That Makes Thinking Fun!"
$5-7

MASTERMIND
Invicta 1972
"Break the Hidden Code"
$3-5

MENTOR
Hasbro 1960's
"The Man of Bronze"
$25-30

CHAOS
Lakeside 1971
Strategy game
$5-7

THE "49ERS"
National Games 1950's
"Game of Risk and Rescue"
$20-25
From the collection of Jeffrey Lowe.

COMPUTER PERFECTION
Lakeside 1979
Electronic version
$7-10

FORTY NINERS
National Games 1950's
$15-20
From the collection of Jeffrey Lowe.

PROSPECTING
Selchow & Righter 1953
"The Gold Rush Game"
$22-25
From the collection of Jeffrey Lowe.

HUNCH
Happy Hour 1956
Marble game in 3-D Plastic
$10-12

PROSPECTING
(Trade Mark)
The Gold Rush Game

Players travel winding mountain
streams searching for "traces" which
perhaps lead to paydirt—the gold nug-
get, novel construction of Prospecting
makes every game different.

No. 58. Prospecting $2.25

Box 15¼″ x 18¼″ x 1½″ with colorful
playing field, having die-cut visual windows
to be opened by players, revolving under—
dial—4 upright wooden pawns, 28 prospecting cards—4 picks—1 catalin die and
directions.

SUPER MARKET
(Trade Mark)
The Red-Light Green-Light
Shopping Game

In Super Market shoppers are limited
to a strict budget which they must
spend for food either in the super
market or neighborhood stores. While
enroute to the shopping areas on foot,
or by taxi, traffic signals must be ob-
served.

No. 56. Super Market $1.00

Box 20″ x 9½″ x 1″ with departmental
super market in cover—neighborhood stores
and traffic light tower in box itself—4 colored wooden pawns, plenty of money, fish,
meat, dairy and vegetable products for all
stores—directions.

BLAST OFF

The Moving Planet Space Ga

An exciting space game—each p
travels through the heavens in a
ette ship—tries to land on the m
planets—attempts to pick up ca
of rare minerals and be the fir
return to earth.

No. 57. Blast Off $

Box 15½″ x 18¼″ x 1½″ with playing
form depicting the heavens and
in which the planets move—4 rockette
20 cargo cards, 6 movable planets,
spinner and directions.

TICKY THE CLOWN CLOCK
Happy Hour 1956
Marble game in 3-D Plastic
$7-10

65

PARCHEESI
Selchow & Righter 1946
Popular Edition
Age old BACKGAMMON style game
$10-15

PARCHEESI
Selchow & Righter 1940's
$20-25

PARCHEESI
Selchow & Righter 1950's
$5-7

PARCHEESI
Selchow & Righter 1950's
Popular Edition
$5

INDIA
Whitman? 1950's
PARCHEESI copy
$3

POLLYANNA
Parker Brothers 1915
(not shown with correct box)
Copy of PARCHEESI
$10- 1 5

POLLYANNA DIXIE
Parker Brothers 1952
$10-12

POLLYANNA
Parker Brothers 1920's (not shown with correct board)
"The Glad Game"
$10-15

POLLYANNA
Parker Brothers 1950's
$10-12

SCRABBLE
Selchow & Righter 1953
Word game, wood tiles
$5-8

SCRABBLE
J.W. Spears & Sons 1955
Plastic Tiles
$8-10

SCRABBLE
J.W. Spears & Sons 1955
$5-7

No. 71 De luxe SCRABBLE Crossword Game

DELUXE SCRABBLE
Selchow & Righter 1953
Revolving Board- Plastic tiles
$10-12

SCRABBLE FOR JUNIORS
Selchow & Righter 1968
Edition three
$2-3

SCRABBLE
Selchow & Righter 1970's
Blanket SCRABBLE-Uncommon
$25-40

MR. REE!
Selchow & Righter 1937
One of forerunners of CLUE
$25-40

RPM
Selchow & Righter 1971
For use with SCRABBLE-
Revolving letter tray forces
you to make words quickly
$10-12

SENTENCE CUBE GAME
Selchow & Righter 1971
$5

MR. REE!
Selchow & Righter 1957
$15

MR. REE!
Selchow & Righter 1937
"The Fireside Detective"
$25- 35

MR. REE!
Selchow & Righter 1946
$20

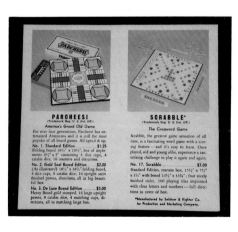

SORRY!
Parker Brothers 1950
Slide Pursuit game
$15-20

SORRY!
Parker Brothers 1964
$5-7

SORRY!
Parker Brothers 1950
"The Great Game"
$10-15

"CLUE"
Parker Brothers 1950
"The Great Detective Game"
$15-20

"CLUE"
Parker Brothers 1963
$5-7

"CLUE"
Parker Brothers 1956
$10-15

"CLUE"
Parker Brothers 1949
$25-35

SORRY!
Parker Brothers 1958
$7-10

"CLUE"
John Waddington Ltd 1949
$30

"CLUE"
Parker Brothers 1949
"The Great New Sherlock Holmes Game!"
$25-40

EASY ON THE KETCHUP GAME
Lakeside 1975
"Lunch Bunch"- Shake out drops
of plastic "Ketchup"- but don't
shake the white drop
$10

KING TUT'S PYRAMID
Milton Bradley 1962
"For the Puzzle Master"
$5-10

HIDE 'N' THIEF
Whitman 1965
"Surprise Game of Hide & Seek"
$10-12

MANHUNT
Milton Bradley 1972
The "Electric Computer
Detective Game"
$10-15

THE F.B.I. GAME
Transogram 1961
Landmark Game Series
$25-35
Courtesy of Rick Polizzi

REBOUND
Ideal 1980
Original version 1971
$5-7

TILT 'N ROLL
Milton Bradley 1964
"Obstacle Puzzle"
$5-10

LOLLI PLOP
Milton Bradley 1962
Skill game
$5-7

STEADY EDDIE
Milton Bradley 1962
"A Balancing Game"
$5-8

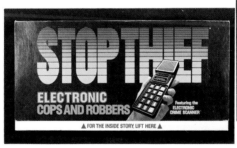

STOP THIEF
Parker Brothers 1979
Featuring the "Electronic
Crime Scanner"
$15-20

CALLING ALL CARS
Parker Brothers 1940's
Metal cars
$12-15

GIANT BARREL OF MONKEYS
Lakeside 1969
$10-15

CAPER
Parker Brothers 1970
"The Great Jewel Robbery Game"
$20-25

ELECTRONIC DETECTIVE
Ideal 1979
"Computerized Who-Done-It Game"
Don Adams on cover- Came with
45 RPM record that explained how
to play the game
$10-15

FBI CRIME RESISTANCE GAME
Milton Bradley 1976
"Crime Resistance Manual Included"
Don't be a Victim!
$10-15

THE WEST POINT STORY GAME
Transogram 1961
Landmark Game Series
$25-35
From the collection of Jeffrey Lowe.

BETSY ROSS AND THE FLAG GAME
Transogram 1961
Landmark Game Series
$25-35
From the collection of Jeffrey Lowe.

THE STORY OF THE U.S. AIR FORCE GAME
Transogram 1961
Landmark Game Series
$35-45
From the collection of Jeffrey Lowe.

THE BLACK EXPERIENCE
Theme Productions 1971
"American History Game"
$10-13
From the collection of Jeffrey Lowe.

MANDINKA
E.S. Lowe 1978
Strategy game
$7-10

SWAHILI GAME
Milton Bradley 1968
Strategy game
$15-20

TRACK & TRAP
Whitman 1969
"The Tiger Hunt Game"
$12-15

SAFARI
Selchow & Righter 1950
"The Great New Hunting Game"
$20

SILLY SAFARI
Topper 1966
Tons of plastic animals
$25-55

BANTU
Parker Brothers 1955
$20-25
From the collection of Jeffrey Lowe.

ANIMAL TRAP GAME
Multiple Products Corp 1950's
Plastic animals
$20-30
From the collection of Jeffrey Lowe.

WILDLIFE
E.S. Lowe 1971
Travel around the world
to collect rare animals for a zoo
$15-20

ANIMAL TALK GAME
Mattel 1963
"Chatty Cathy" ring
provides 12 animal sounds
$25-30
From the collection of Jeffrey Lowe.

SUNKEN TREASURE
Milton Bradley 1976
works like OPERATION
$12-15

SUNKEN TREASURE GAME
Parker Brothers 1948
Track game
$15-20

GEO-GRAPHY WORLD WIDE
Cadaco-Ellis 1954
Educational game-there was
a companion game called
TOP-OGRAPHY
$15-18

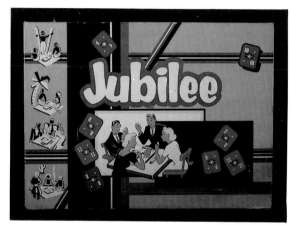

SPLIT LEVEL AGGRAVATION
Lakeside 1971
A three dimensional version of an old favorite.

JUBILEE
Cadaco-Ellis 1954
Tile game
$15-20

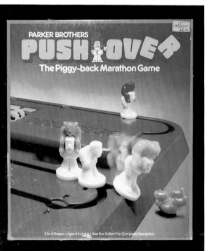

TOP SCHOLAR
Cadaco-Ellis 1957
"World-Wide Knowledge Game"
$15-20
From the collection of Jeffrey Lowe.

PROJECT CIA
Waddington 1973
"A Spy Training Game"
$10

PUSH OVER
Parker Brothers 1981
$5-7

QUIZ PANEL
Cadaco-Ellis 1954
$10-15
From the collection of Jeffrey Lowe.

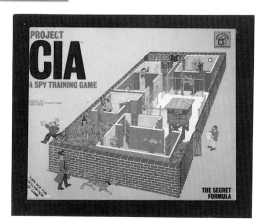

GREEN GHOST GAME
Transogram 1965
Large game glows in the dark
$45-75

ZOK
Hasbro 1967
Giant vinyl playing mat
$10

CASCADE
Matchbox 1972
The "Thump-A-Drum" Game
$10-15

CLOCK-A-WORD
Topper 1966
Weird word game-Companion game
called CLOCK-A-GAME
$10-12

POPCORN
Marx Toys 1976
"Catch Your Color Balls and Win!"
$12-15

KNOCK IT OFF GAME
Marx Toys 1978
"Wacky Street Game"
$7

AMERICAN PACHINKO
Pressman 1970's
$20

SLEEP WALKER
Kenner 1976
"Featuring Sleepwalkin' Sam"
$10

LANDSLIDE
Parker Brothers 1971
"Power Politics"
$10-12

LOBBY
Milton Bradley 1949
"A Capital Game"
$20-25
Courtesy of Toy Scouts, Inc

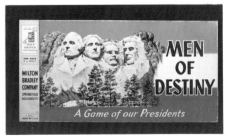

MEN OF DESTINY
Milton Bradley 1956
"A Game of our Presidents"
$15-20

FLAGSHIP AIRFREIGHT
Milton Bradley 1946
The Airline Cargo Game"
$30-40
From the collection of Jeffrey Lowe.

FERRY COMMAND
Milton Bradley 1943
"The Flying Fortress Game"
$25-30
From the collection of Jeffrey Lowe.

FLYING THE BEAM
Parker Brothers 1941
"A Game of Aerial Transport"
$20-25

3 POINT LANDING
Advance Games Co 1940's
Air race game
$20-25
From the collection of Jeffrey Lowe.

HAPPY LANDING
Transogram 1938
"Made for Brother and Sister
Played by Mother and Dad"
$20
From the collection of Jeffrey Lowe.

FLIGHT CAPTAIN
E.S. Lowe 1972
Plays like TROUBLE
$10-15
From the collection of Jeffrey Lowe.

ASTRON
Parker Brothers 1955
"The Game That Moves as You Play"
$25-30
From the collection of Jeffrey Lowe.

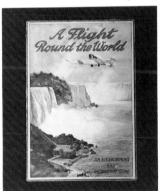

A FLIGHT ROUND THE WORLD
Spears 1928
Metal planes
$25-45

GAME OF STATE CAPTITALS
Parker Brothers 1952
"How Many State Capitals Can You
Name? "
$7-10

MT. EVEREST
Gabriel 1955
3-D game-
"Climb the Highest
Mountain"
$25-30
From the collection of Jeffrey Lowe.

CARGOES
(Trademark Reg. U. S. Pat. Off.)
The Seafaring Travel Game

Adventurous travels all over the world to obtain valuable cargoes of precious gems, spices, foodstuffs, etc. The successful captain will stay with his ship and fight terrific storms, gales, and fog to bring his cargo safely to port— thrilling, exciting. For 2 to 4 players. Ages—7 and up.

No. 42. Cargoes **$2.25**
Colorful box 16½" x 10" x 2", containing 5-panel folding World Map Board, showing principal seaports, 4 miniature ships, 1 die, 1 dice cup, 40 consignment cards, 66 cargo cards, directions.

EMBOSSED ANAGRAMS

Anagrams is an outstanding favorite with young and old alike. These anagrams are the finest made — large maple blocks — excellent finish — eye resting colors.

No. 79. Anagrams **$1.25**
Box 6½" x 6½" x 1½" containing 90 beautifully embossed blocks.

HUGGIN' THE RAIL
(Trademark Reg. U. S. Pat. Off.)
The Realistic Auto Race Game

There's no hogging the game in HUGGIN' THE RAIL because the LANE-LOCATOR will swing a racer from the inside lane to the outside and it's really a battle for position right up to the exciting finish line. Any number can play. All ages, 6 and up.

No. 46. Huggin' the Rail **$2.25**
Packed in attractive colorful box 16½" x 10" x 1½" with 3 panel folding board depicting circular speedway. Novel Lane-Locator, 1 large die, 6 metal racing cars in colors, and directions.

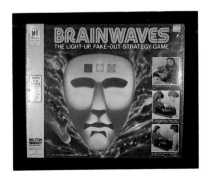

BRAIN WAVES
Milton Bradley 1977
"Fake-Out Strategy Game"
$5-7

LOTTO 6/4 ALL
L.L. Ltd 1989
California Edition
Pick Lotto numbers by
throwing sticky balls at
numbered chart
$3

BALAROO
Milton Bradley 1967
Fine Edition
$10-12

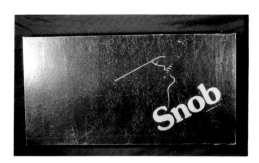

SNOB
Helene Fox Inc 1983
$7-10

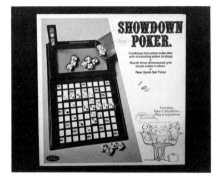

SHOWDOWN POKER
E.S. Lowe 1971
Dice/Poker
$5-7

DOLLAR BILL POKER
E.S. Lowe 1974
Tony Randall & Jack Klugman
as "Odd Couple" on cover
$5

CHUTE-5
E.S. Lowe 1973
Strategy dice game
$5-7

PIRATE'S ISLAND
Corey Games 1942
"A Game of Adventure"
$25-35
From the collection of Jeffrey Lowe.

PIRATE AND TRAVELER
Milton Bradley 1936
"Greatest of All Games"
$20

TRADE WINDS
Parker Brothers 1960
"Caribbean Sea Game"
$20-25

TREASURE HUNT
Cadaco-Ellis 1942
23rd Edition
$10

JINGO
Cadaco-Ellis 1941
"The Jigsaw Bingo Game"
$10-15

PIRATE AND TRAVELER
Milton Bradley 1960
$10

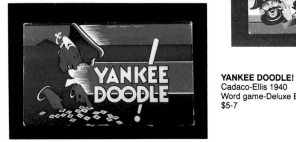

TREASURE HUNT
Cadaco-Ellis 1950
$5

YANKEE DOODLE!
Cadaco-Ellis 1940
Word game-Deluxe Edition 15
$5-7

LOST GOLD
Parker Brothers 1975
With unique "Gold Finder"
$12-15

GETAWAY CHASE GAME
DX(AMF) 1960's
Cross between slot car racing
and board game
$40-65

BIG TOWN
Milton Bradley 1962
"A Live Action Game"
$25-35
Courtesy of Rick Polizzi.

RACE TRAP
Multiple Toymakers 1960's
Steer "Wild Willy" through
the correct gateway
$30-40

GET THAT LICENSE
Selchow & Righter 1955
"The License Plate Game"
$15-18

TAXI!
Selchow & Righter 1960
Revamped CABBY
$12-15
From the collection of Jeffrey Lowe.

CABBY!
Selchow & Righter 1940's
Popular game with the
"Rules Made to be Broken!"
$25-32

INTERSTATE HIGHWAY
Selchow & Righter 1963
Travel game
$25-35
From the collection of Jeffrey Lowe.

TRAFFIC JAM
Harett-Gilmar, Inc 1954
Plastic traffic signs
$25-35
From the collection of Jeffrey Lowe.

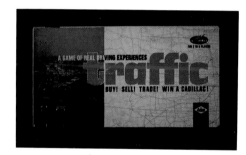

TRAFFIC
E.S. Lowe 1968
Game of "Real Driving
Experiences"
$12-15

THE MAGNIFICENT RACE
Parker Brothers 1975
Travel game
$7-10

GAME OF HAPPINESS
Milton Bradley 1972
"Mod" art and plastic
pieces
$12-15

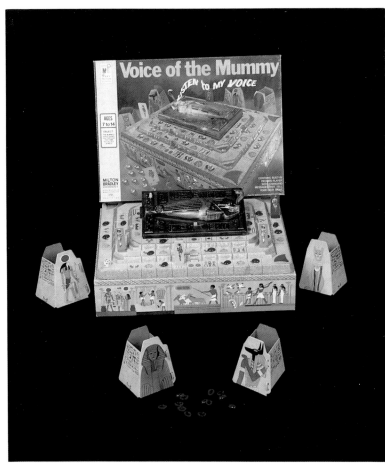

VOICE OF THE MUMMY
Milton Bradley 1971
"Listen to My Voice"-
Players collected jewels as they
raced around the Mummy's sarcophagus- If
they landed on a space that required them
to listen to the Mummy's voice, a tiny record
player concealed in his tomb usually spelled
out disaster. SEANCE was a sequel to this game.

MOUSE TRAP GAME
Ideal 1963
The classic game- Actually
a Rube Goldberg-esque toy that
became a game...and a hit-
A Marvin Glass design
$35-45

MOUSE TRAP GAME
Ideal 1975
$10

THE BOSS
Ideal 1972
"Firing the Boss is all
Part of the Fun!"
$10-20
From the collection of Jeffrey Lowe.

FISH BAIT GAME
Ideal 1965
Third and most unsuccessful
copy of MOUSE TRAP-
Marvin Glass design
$25- 3 0

CRAZY CLOCK GAME
Ideal 1964
Sequel to MOUSE TRAP-
Marvin Glass design
$25-40

ROMAN X
Selchow & Righter 1964
"The Game of Caesars"
$10-15
From the collection of Jeffrey Lowe.

BRUCE FORCE
Ideal 1963
"And the Treasure of
Shark Island"- From an "Envelope
Series" of games- Also "Bruce Force:
Lost in Outer Space"
$20-25
Courtesy of Rick Polizzi.

LIZ TYLER
Ideal 1963
"Hollywood Starlet"
Envelope Series
$15-20

LIZ TYLER
Ideal 1963
"And the Mystery of the
Crown Jewels"
Envelope Series
$15-20

CROW HUNT
Parker Brothers 1940's
With Daisy rifle
$35-45
From the collection of Jeffrey Lowe.

HIPPETY-HOP
Corey Games 1940
Weird game
$25-35
From the collection of Jeffrey Lowe.

MAGIC! MAGIC! MAGIC! GAME
Remco 1975
Game where you perform tricks
$15-20

GOING TO JERUSALEM
Parker Brothers 1955
"Bible Game Based on the New
Testament"
$20-25

CHUTZPAH
What-Cha-Ma-Call-It Inc 1967
"$10, But for you...$5.95"
$7-10

BARGAIN HUNTER
Milton Bradley 1981
Featuring a "Plastic Credit
Card Machine"
$10-12

CHARGE IT!
Whitman 1972
Card game-"Be the First
to Accumulate the Most Wealth...
On Credit!"
$7-10

77

THE GAME OF HOLLYWOOD STARS
Whitman 1955
$10

GOING HOLLYWOOD
Hollywood Game Co 1943
$25-35
From the collection of Jeffrey Lowe.

SUS-PENSE
Northwestern Products 1950's
Hangman game
$10-14
From the collection of Jeffrey Lowe.

SHOW-BIZ
Lowell 1950's
"The Game of the Stars"
$25-35
From the collection of Jeffrey Lowe.

"MEXICAN PETE"
Parker Brothers 1940's
"I Got It", although I'm
not sure what "It" is
$15-20
From the collection of Jeffrey Lowe.

SWINGIN' SAM
Peerless Playthings Co 1960's
Hangman game
$10

DIRECTOR'S CHOICE
Direct Broadcast Programs Inc 1984
A video tape was included with
this movie trivia game
$7-10

THE GAME OF RIO
Parker Brothers 1956
$20-25

HANGMAN
Milton Bradley 1976
Vincent Price on cover
$5-7

THE GAME OF LIFE
Milton Bradley 1960
Has "100th Anniversary Game"
on cover
$15-20

THE GAME OF LIFE
Milton Bradley 1960's
$5-10

SHADOWLORD!
Parker Brothers 1983
Dungeons/Dragons theme
$8-10

KING OF THE MOUNTAIN
Saalfield 1957
"Race to the Mountain Top-
Win the King's Crown"
$10-15
From the collection of Jeffrey Lowe.

BIG FOOT
Milton Bradley 1977
The "Giant Snow Monster"
smiles benignly as the
youngsters play his game
$10

OIL THE GREAT ADVENTURE
J & L Randall 1960's
Drill for oil
$20-25
From the collection of Jeffrey Lowe.

LIGHTNING EXPRESS
Milton Bradley 1940's
"A Railroad Game"
$25-30
From the collection of Jeffrey Lowe.

TRAVEL
Gardner Games 1960's
Travel game
$12-15

TIN CAN ALLEY
Ideal 1976
Electronic rifle knocks over
Dr. Pepper cans-Chuck Connors
on cover
$25-45

BLIZZARD OF '77
C.P. Marino 1977
Travel Game
$7-10

CAN-DOO
Aurora 1970's
Try to remove stacked
Campbell's soup cans without
toppling them
$10-15

TIE 'N TANGLE
Hasbro 1967
TWISTER-esque game
$15-20

AERO-BALL
Game Makers Inc 1940's
Skill game
$7-10
From the S. Becdach Collection.

TEEKO
John Scarne Games Inc 1952
"America's Most Fascinating Game"
$10

AIRLINE
Mulgara Products 1985
World travel game
$7-9

79

BASH!
Milton Bradley 1965
Players stacked up the plastic
pieces that formed his body- then
took turns trying to Bash the
sections out, one at a time, with included
hammer. Came with Oh Fooey! card to get a free
turn.

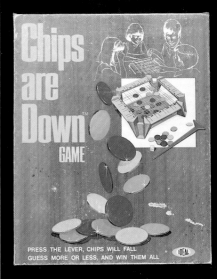

CHIPS ARE DOWN GAME
Ideal 1970
Chip guessing game
$10-15

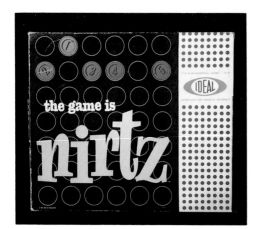

THE GAME IS NIRTZ
Ideal 1961
$10

BLITZ
Dynamic Games 1972
Game of chance
$7-9

MARBLE-HEAD GAME
Ideal 1969
Similar to KER-PLUNK
$20-25

S-S-S-SCAT
Cadaco 1967
"A Thrilling Game of
Reflexes"
$5-7

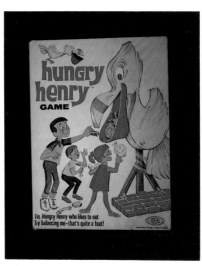

HUNGRY HENRY GAME
Ideal 1969
Balancing game
$20

WHAT SHALL I BE?
Selchow & Righter 1966
Career game for girls
$10-14

WHAT SHALL I WEAR?
Selchow & Righter 1969
Fashion game for girls
$10
From the collection of Jeffrey Lowe.

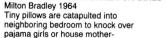

WOW PILLOW FIGHT GAME FOR GIRLS
Milton Bradley 1964
Tiny pillows are catapulted into
neighboring bedroom to knock over
pajama girls or house mother-
Another game called POW! CANNON
GAME FOR BOYS was made-Marvin Glass design
$20-25

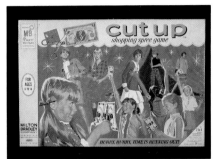

CUT UP SHOPPING SPREE GAME
Milton Bradley 1968
Bizzare game in which players
cut out money (with included scissors)
to buy displayed items before time runs
out- Marvin Glass design
$20-27

MYSTERY DATE GAME
Milton Bradley 1965
Very popular game
"Is Your Date Behind This Door?"
Marvin Glass design
$25-30

MISS POPULARITY GAME
Transogram 1961
"The Game all Girls Love to Play"
Marvin Glass design
$20-30

PATHFINDER
Milton Bradley 1954
Tile strategy game
$10-12
From the collection of Jeffrey Lowe.

PATHFINDER
Milton Bradley 1977
No one knows why David
Janssen appears to be on the cover
$7

GAME OF FOX AND HOUNDS
Parker Brothers 1948
Chase game-Metal pieces
$15-20

LIE DETECTOR
Mattel 1960
Solve crimes using the
"Official Lie Detector
$20-25

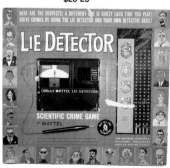

DEALER'S CHOICE
Parker Brothers1972
Car Card game
Marvin Glass design
$12-15

SALUTE!
Selchow & Righter 1940's
Wooden pieces
$25-30
From the collection of Jeffrey Lowe.

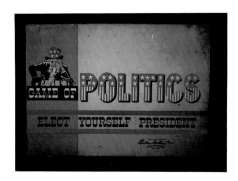

COURTROOM
W. Roy Tribble 1970's
"The American Game of Law"
$7-10

TRIAL LAWYER
James N. Vail 1977
"The Jurisprudence Game"
$5-7

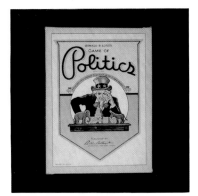

OSWALD B. LORD'S GAME OF POLITICS
Parker Brothers 1930's
(Board not shown)
$25-35

GAME OF POLITICS
Parker Brothers 1952
"Elect Yourself President"
$20-25

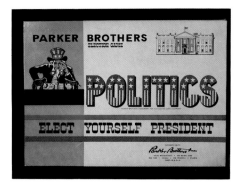

POLITICS
Parker Brothers 1960
$20

MEET THE PRESIDENTS
Selchow & Righter 1950
Gold or Silver coins with President's
visages on them
$20- 25

SCARNE'S CHALLENGE
Scarne's Challenge 1947
Created by the "World's Foremost
Game Authority"
$7-10
From the collection of Jeffrey Lowe.

SKIP-A-CROSS
Cadaco-Ellis 1954
"Licensed by the Makers of
SCRABBLE"-
$10-15

MEET THE PRESIDENTS
Tied to the trend of the Times

It teaches youngsters historical facts about every President from Washington to Eisenhower. The more history you know, the faster your Presidents reach the White House. Contains 33 beautiful coins children will keep as collector's item. For ages 8 and up.
No. 40. MEET THE PRESIDENTS $3.50
Beautiful cellophane window box 14¾"x10" x1½". Map Board 19½"x14¼" of U.S. with historical pathways. 33 Aluminum Presidential coins and giant 9" die-cut Question and Answer Spinner.

DEAD PAN
Trademark
The Game of Wits

Just like eating Peanuts — when you play Dead Pan, you keep coming back for more. Another Winner following on the heels of Scrabble. Novel in appearance, new in method of play and easy—so easy to learn. Nothing to do but drop Marbles into the beautiful plastic trays—but it's a real Challenge to WIN. For all ages.
No. 50. DEAD PAN $3.00
In beautiful modern box 16½"x9¾"x2", containing four colored plastic trays, 72 colored marbles, short easy-to-read directions in box cover.

[PRICES HIGHER WEST OF THE MISSISSIPPI AND IN CANADA]

FLASH
Selchow & Righter 1956
"The Press Photographer's Game"
$20-25
From the collection of Jeffrey Lowe.

THE GAMES PEOPLE PLAY GAME
Alpsco 1967
Based on the book by Eric Berne
$7-10
From the collection of Jeffrey Lowe.

MERRY MILKMAN EXCITING GAME AND TOY
Hasbro 1955
Milk trucks and Cardboard houses
$25-35

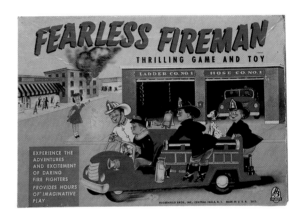

FEARLESS FIREMAN THRILLING GAME & TOY
Hasbro 1955
"Provides Hours of Imaginative Play"
$35-40
Courtesy of Rick Polizzi.

KER PLUNK
Ideal 1967
"A Tantalizing Game of Nerve and Skill". Remove Toothpicks one at a time until the marbles start to drop. Similar to MARBLE HEAD.

OPERATION SKILL GAME
Milton Bradley 1965
"Where You're the Doctor"
$10-14

POLICE PATROL ACTION GAME AND TOY
Hasbro 1955
Game and Toy series
Large plastic pieces
$35-40
Courtesy of Rick Polizzi.

MR. DOODLE'S DOG
Selchow & Righter 1950's
Track game-Created by Howard R. Garis,
who created UNCLE WIGGILY
$15-20
From the collection of Jeffrey Lowe.

POOCH
Hasbro 1954
$15-20
From the collection of Jeffrey Lowe.

THE RED ROVER GAME
Cadaco 1963
$10-15
From the collection of Jeffrey Lowe.

LOT THE CALF
Brown Games Inc 1964
Strategy game
$15-20
From the collection of Jeffrey Lowe.

LITTLE BOY BLUE
Cadaco-Ellis 1955
Game of "Hide and Go Seek"
$10-15
From the collection of Jeffrey Lowe.

THE CHASE
Cadaco 1966
"A Nature Study Game"
Unusual perspective cover
$12-15
From the collection of Jeffrey Lowe.

SPIDER AND THE FLY
Whitman 1962
Skill game
$10-12

DECOY
Selchow & Righter 1956
Plastic Ducks
$20-25
From the collection of Jeffrey Lowe.

OVER THE GARDEN WALL
Milton Bradley 1937
Skill game
$8-10

THIS GAME IS BONKERS!
Parker Brothers 1978
"It's Never the Same Game Twice"
$8-10

HICKETY PICKETY
Parker Brothers 1954
$8-10
Wooden eggs
From the collection of Jeffrey Lowe.

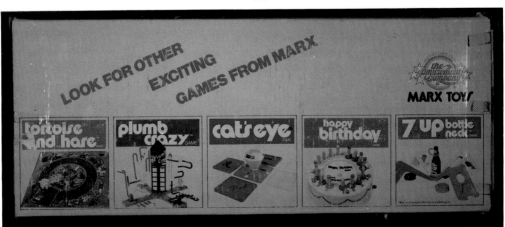

HI-Q
Tryne 1950's
Puzzle game
$3-5

HI-Q
Kohner 1960's
$2-3

BREAKING POINT
Ideal 1976
Skill game
$5-7

DOMINATION
Milton Bradley 1982
Strategy game
$5-7

BLOCK THE CLOCK
Ideal 1981
Arrange track for swiftly
moving clock
$8-10

ROLLER COASTER
Milton Bradley 1973
Skill game
$7-10

KABOOM BALLOON BUSTING GAME
Ideal 1965
Similar to BLOWOUT-Don't
over-fill the balloon
$19-22

STAY ALIVE GAME
Milton Bradley 1971
"The Ultimate Survival Game"
$7-10

ON GUARD
Parker Brothers 1967
Skill game
$7-9

THINK-THUNK
Milton Bradley 1973
"Strategy Action Game"
$10-12

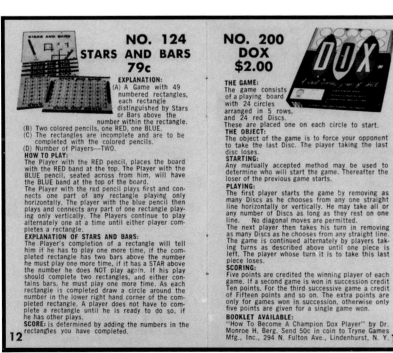

STARS AND BARS

NO. 124
STARS AND BARS
79c

EXPLANATION:
(A) A Game with 49 numbered rectangles, each rectangle distinguished by Stars or Bars above the number within the rectangle.
(B) Two colored pencils, one RED, one BLUE.
(C) The rectangles are incomplete and are to be completed with the colored pencils.
(D) Number of Players—TWO.

HOW TO PLAY:
The Player with the RED pencil, places the board with the RED band at the top. The Player with the BLUE pencil, seated across from him, will have the BLUE band at the top of the board.
The Player with the red pencil plays first and connects one part of any rectangle playing only horizontally. The player with the blue pencil then plays and connects any part of one rectangle playing only vertically. The Players continue to play alternately one at a time until either player completes a rectangle.

EXPLANATION OF STARS AND BARS:
The Player's completion of a rectangle will tell him if he has to play one more time, if the completed rectangle has two bars above the number he must play one more time, if it has a STAR above the number he does NOT play again. If his play should complete two rectangles, and either contains bars, he must play one more time. As each rectangle is completed draw a circle around the number in the lower right hand corner of the completed rectangle. A player does not have to complete a rectangle until he is ready to do so, if he has other plays.
SCORE: is determined by adding the numbers in the rectangles you have completed.

12

NO. 200
DOX
$2.00

THE GAME:
The game consists of a playing board with 24 circles arranged in 5 rows, and 24 red Discs. These are placed one on each circle to start.
THE OBJECT:
The object of the game is to force your opponent to take the last Disc. The player taking the last disc loses.
STARTING:
Any mutually accepted method may be used to determine who will start the game. Thereafter the loser of the previous game starts.
PLAYING:
The first player starts the game by removing as many Discs as he chooses from any one straight line horizontally or vertically. He may take all or any number of Discs as they rest on one line.   No diagonal moves are permitted.
The next player then takes his turn in removing as many Discs as he chooses from any straight line. The game is continued alternately by players taking turns as described above until one piece is left. The player whose turn it is to take this last piece loses.
SCORING:
Five points are credited the winning player of each game. If a second game is won in succession credit Ten points. For the third successive game a credit of Fifteen points and so on. The extra points are only for games won in succession, otherwise only five points are given for a single game won.
BOOKLET AVAILABLE:
"How To Become A Champion Dox Player" by Dr. Monroe H. Berg. Send 50c in coin to Tryne Games Mfg., Inc., 294 N. Fulton Ave., Lindenhurst, N. Y.

13

HIP FLIP
Parker Brothers 1968
"Swinging Game for Swinging People"
Marvin Glass design
$20-25

85

INTRIGUE
Milton Bradley 1955
Game plays similar to CLUE. Wooden satchels,
metal keys to staterooms and a "dead body"
heighten the action, all aboard an ocean liner.

NORTHWEST PASSAGE!
Impact Communications 1969
Commemorating Humble's "Maiden
Northwest Passage Voyage"
$20-22
From the collection of Jeffrey Lowe.

BERMUDA TRIANGLE GAME
Milton Bradley 1976
A moving "Sinister Mystery
Cloud" swallows unwary ships-
Neat game
$15-20

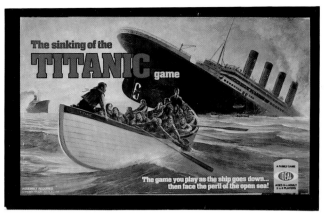

THE SINKING OF THE TITANIC GAME
Ideal 1976
"The Game You Play as the Ship Goes
Down...Then Face the Peril of the
Open Sea!"- Upbeat game
$12-15

JET RACE GAME
Built-Rite 1960's
"Speed" game
$8-12

INTERNATIONAL AIRPORT GAME
Magic Wand 1964
Magnetic game-Same series
as COMBAT TANK
$12-15
From the collection of Jeffrey Lowe.

AROUND THE WORLD TRAVEL GAME
Golden Rock Co 1975
Travel game
$10 12

RRIB-BIT
Genesis Enterprises 1973
Plastic Frogs as Chess pieces
$10-15

SMESS THE NINNY'S CHESS
Parker Brothers 1970
Weird Chess-like game
$10-12

ALL THE KING'S MEN
Parker Brothers 1979
Could be revamped CAMELOT
$8-10

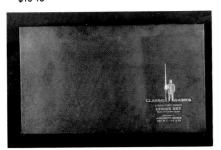

CLASSIC GAMES CHESS SET
Classic Games Co 1963
"Collector's Series"
Different Editions of Chess
sets were put out, this one
being figures from Ancient Rome
$20-30

MAH-JONGG GAME
Manufacturer Unknown 1920's
When "MAH-JONGG" fever hit the
U.S. in the 1920's a multitude of
differently titled sets were imported
until government action stemmed the
tide-This set has ivory/bamboo pieces
$35-55

MAH-JONGG "JUNIOR"
Mah-Jongg Sales of America 1923
Wood set
$8-10

MAN-CHU
U.S. Playing Card Co 1923
"The Famous Chinese Game"
MAH-JONGG with cards
$15-20

1-2-3 GAME HOT SPOT!
Parker Brothers 1961
"A New Game for a New Age"
$15-20
From the collection of Jeffrey Lowe.

DOUBLE TROUBLE SUPER PUZZLE GAME
Whitman 1968
Puzzle game
$5-6

SITUATION7
Parker Brothers 1969
"Space Puzzle Game"
$10-12

PARCHEESI
(Trademark Reg. U.S. Pat. Off.)
America's Grand Old Game
For over four generations, Parcheesi
has entertained Americans and it is
still the most popular of all board
games. All ages—6 and up.
No. 1. Standard Edition **$1.25**
Folding board 18½" x 18½", box of implements 6½" x 3" containing 4 dice cups,
dice, 16 counters and directions.
No. 2. De Luxe Edition **$2.25**
Heavy board—16 upright pawns—4 catalin
dice.
No. 3. Boxed Edition **$3.00**
16 upright pawns, 8 catalin dice—beautifully boxed.

SCRABBLE*
(Trademark Reg. U.S. Pat. Off.)
The Crossword Game
Scrabble is a fascinating word game
with a scoring feature—and it's so
easy to learn. Once played, old and
young alike, experience a tantalizing
challenge to play it again and again.
No. 17. Scrabble **$3.00**
Standard Edition — maroon box — 15½" x
7½" x 1½" with board 14½" x 14¼"—4
nicely finished racks, 100 playing tiles im-
printed with clear letters and numbers—full
directions in cover of box.
* **Manufactured by Selchow & Righter Co.
for Production and Marketing Corp.**

CABBY
(Trademark Reg. U.S. Pat. Off.)
*The Game With Rules
Made To Be Broken*
This is a game packed with fun—the
alert police cars are waiting for any
traffic violations so they can invoke
the penalties. The arrests and escapes
plus getting your cab customers to
their proper destinations is really exciting. Four can play. Ages—7 and up.
No. 16. Cabby **$1.75**
Packed in attractive streamlined box 20" x
9½" with 4 metal police cars—4
metal taxicabs, 2 dice, 28 passengers and
complete directions.

DUNGEON DICE
Parker Brothers 1977
Dice game
$5-6

87

BINGO OR BEANO A GAME
Parker Brothers 1930's
Bingo game
$7-10

3 HOURS OF PARTY FUN AND GAMES
Transogram 1955
Popular Edition
With "Stunts and Pranks Galore"
$7-9

WIPE OFF TARGET GAME
Milton Bradley 1959
Similar to BATTLESHIP
$5-8

DELUXE BINGO
Whitman 1957
With "Magic Dispenser"
$4-5

JOLLYTIME DOMINOES
Milton Bradley 1955
Picture or regular DOMINOES
$8

WINNER SPINNER
Whitman 1953
$5-7

PRESSMAN BINGO
Pressman 1960's
Metal spinner
$3-5

THE CHILDREN'S HOUR
Parker Brothers 1950's
"3 Good Games of 20 Minutes Each"
That's one hour or "A Laugh a Minute"-
Includes "Porky the Pig"
$8-10

FLIP FOR FUN
Parker Brothers 1966
"Play in the Car With Seat
Belts Buckled"
$2-3

BLOCKHEAD!
Saalfield 1954
Wooden blocks-Common game
$5-7

CAMELOT A "jumping game" particularly suited to men and boys. It affords a wide field of strategy for serious players. It is like neither checkers or chess but is livelier with more exciting climaxes. This game has many ardent devotees. Attractive board and nicely finished pieces.

CHILDREN'S HOUR A collection of three delightful games especially designed to amuse young boys and girls. These games, Peanut the Elephant, Porky the Pig and ABC Fishing are elementary without complicated moves. Interesting little animals, spinner, cards and board.

MAGNETIC FISH POND
Milton Bradley 1942
One of a million fish pond
games
$7-10

RUMMY ROYAL
Whitman 1959
"Sometimes Called 'Michigan'"
$3-4

LUCKY SNAP BALL
Milton Bradley 1941
Skill game
$10-15

COMPLETE TIDDLEDY WINKS
Parker Brothers 1962
5 different ways to play
$5-7

CRIBBAGE BOARD
Milton Bradley 1960's
$2-3

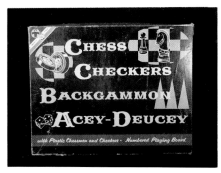

CHESS CHECKERS BACKGAMMON ACEY-DEUCEY
Transogram 1960
$5-7

2 GAME PLAY-TRAY
Transogram 1959
For "Michigan Rummy and
Ace-Hi Horse Race"
$5

BRADLEY'S FIVE SPOT
Milton Bradley 1931
"A Novel Game of Pool"
$12-15
From the collection of Jeffrey Lowe.

CHING CONG ORIENTAL CHECKERS
Samuel Gabriel Sons & Co 1930's
Chinese checkers
$10-15

SPACE CHECKERS
Pacific Game Co 1971
3-D Checkers
$5-7

CHESS CHECKERS & ACEY DEUCY BACKGAMMON
Milton Bradley 1970
$3-5

CHECKERUMMY
Adams Mfg & Supply Co 1946
Cross between Rummy and guess
what...
$2-4

TIDDLY WINKS
Whitman 1950's
$5

GAME OF TIT TAT TOE MARBLE GAME
Parker Brothers 1930's
"3 in a Row"
Wooden skill game
$12-15

TEXAS CHECKERS
Azco 1960's
Giant Checkers
$3-5

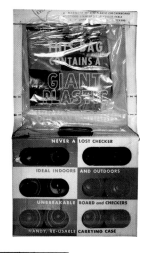

CHECKLINE
Crestline Mfg & Supply Co 1960's
"The Classic Space Tic-Tac-Toe Game"
$5-6

89

CHARLES GOREN'S ADVANCED BRIDGE FOR ONE
Milton Bradley 1967
Fine Edition
$5-7

GOREN'S BRIDGE FOR TWO
Milton Bradley 1964
$3-7

CHARLES GOREN'S CUTTHROAT BRIDGE FOR THREE
Milton Bradley 1968
Fine Edition
$3-5

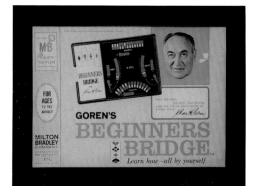

GOREN'S BEGINNER'S BRIDGE
Milton Bradley 1967
$4-5

CHARLES GOREN'S PLAY AND DEFEND BRIDGE
Milton Bradley 1965
Fine Edition
$4-5

CHARLES GOREN'S ROLOMATIC BRIDGE MACHINE
Milton Bradley 1969
"Set II for Experienced Players"
$7-9

AUTO BRIDGE
The Auto Bridge Co 1948
$3-5

BRIDGE KENO
Milton Bradley 1930
Forerunner of PO-KE-NO
$5-7

PO-KE-NO
U.S. Playing Card Co 1960's
Poker Keno
$5-8

PEGITY AND OTHER GAMES
Parker Brothers 1953
Strategy game
$5-9

"NOGGIN"
Tru-Craft 1955
"The Game That Spells Backward"
$7-10

SKUDO
Parker Brothers 1949
"The Turn-Table Game"
$12-15
From the collection of Jeffrey Lowe.

SCORE FOUR
Funtastic 1968
Strategy game
$5-6

SPIN-O
Corey Games 1942
"Top Scoring Game"
$20-25

GAME OF SKATTERBUG
Parker Brothers 1951
Spinning game
$15-20
From the collection of Jeffrey Lowe.

SCRIBBAGE
E.S. Lowe 1963
Word game
$5-6

TWIN SCRIBBAGE
E.S. Lowe 1965
$5-6

KISMET
Lakeside 1964
"The Modern Game of Yacht"
$5-7

MILLE BORNES
Edmond Dujardin 1960
"American Model"
Similar to TOURING
$5-7

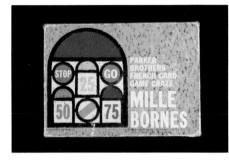

MILLE BORNES
Parker Brothers 1962
$5

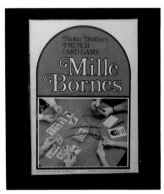

MILLE BORNES
Parker Brothers 1971
$3

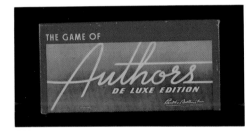

THE GAME OF AUTHORS
Parker Brothers 1942
"De Luxe Edition"
$5-7

THE GAME OF JACK STRAWS
Parker Brothers 1900's
$5

MOUSIE-MOUSIE
Spears Games 1963
"Catch 'Em as They Run"
$5-7

GLOBE-TROTTERS
(Patent Pending)
The World Travel Game with "The Range Finder"

Travel to strange lands the world over. Visit many places with the whole family and make geography real fun. It's exciting and entertaining to circle the globe by plane, ship or train. No two trips are the same. See if you can get home free of debt. Two to four players. Ages—9 and up.
No. 44. Globe-Trotters.........$3.00
Colorful box 21″ x 10½″ x 1¼″ containing beautiful lithographed true-scale, polar-projected world map board 20¼″ x 20¼″, plastic range finder, one ½″ die, 4 markers, script money, 38 chance cards, 24 continent cards and full directions.

WEST OF THE MISSISSIPPI AND IN CANADA)

HOME TEAM BASEBALL
A World Series of Fun

Take a healthy swing and make a double, triple or Home Run. This game is a *Hit* with young and old alike. The umpire makes the decisions just like Big League Baseball. Tight games, errors, stolen bases, and exciting 9th inning rallies have everyone rooting to the end of the game. 18 may play. For ages 7 and up.

No. 25. Home Team Baseball......$1
Beautiful box 20″ x 9½″ x 1″, containing lithographed diamond, 3 action spinners, The Batter, The Fielder, The Umpire, and 20 colored wood player counters.

SNAKE EYES
(Trademark Reg. U. S. Pat. Off.)
The Lively Party Game

It's easy—it's fast. Just the right kind of game for your next "party success." Roll out the dice—turn down the cards—pick up the chips. Plenty of action all the time. No complicated rules. Five can play—for older children and adults.

No. 27. Snake Eyes........$1.50
Beautiful compartment box 11″ x 7¼″ x 1½″, 5 decks of humorous cards, plenty of bone chips, 1 pair catalin dice, 1 dice cup, and directions.

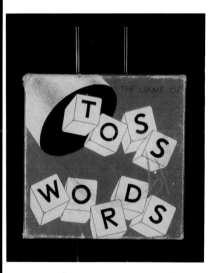

THE GAME OF TOSSWORDS
Kraeg Games 1948
$4-5

RACKO
Milton Bradley 1961
Card game- There is an
original edition
$6-8

RACK-O
Parker Brothers 1966
$4

SUPER RACK-O GAME
Parker Brothers 1983
$5

VENTURE
3M 1968
"3M Card Game Series"
$5-7

TRYCE
3M 1969
"3M Card Game Series"
$5-7

VENTURE
3M 1969
$5

SKIP-BO CARD GAME
Skip-Bo Co 1967
Original Edition
$7-10

QUICK WIT
Parker Brothers 1938
Card game-Gluyas Williams Cover
$12-15

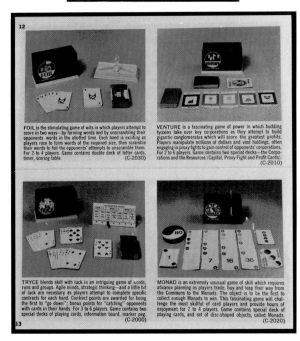

FOIL is the stimulating game of wits in which players attempt to score in two ways—by forming words and by unscrambling their opponents words in the allotted time. Each hand is exciting as players race to form words of the required size, then scramble their words to foil the opponents' attempts to unscramble them. For 2 to 4 players. Game contains double deck of letter cards, timer, scoring table. (C-2030)

VENTURE is a fascinating game of power in which budding tycoons take over key corporations as they attempt to build gigantic conglomerates which will score the greatest profits. Players manipulate millions of dollars and vast holdings, often engaging in proxy fights to gain control of opponents' corporations. For 2 to 6 players. Game contains two special decks—the Corporations and the Resources (Capital, Proxy Fight and Profit Cards). (C-2010)

TRYCE blends skill with luck in an intriguing game of words, runs and groups. Agile minds, strategic thinking—and a little bit of luck are necessary as players attempt to complete specific contracts for each hand. Contract points are awarded for being the first to "go down"; bonus points for "catching" opponents with cards in their hands. For 3 to 6 players. Game contains two special decks of playing cards, information board, marker peg. (C-2000)

MONAD is an extremely unusual game of skill which requires advance planning as players trade, buy and leap their way from the Commons to the Monads. The object is to be the first to collect enough Monads to win. This fascinating game will challenge the most skillful of card players and provide hours of enjoyment for 2 to 4 players. Game contains special deck of playing cards, and set of disc-shaped objects, called Monads. (C-2020)

KAN-U-GO
A.A. Burnstine Sales 1937
Crossword card game
$5-8

CONTACK
Parker Brothers 1930's
Triangle Matching game
$5

NEVER SAY DIE
Parker Brothers 1959
Dice game
$5-7

HEARTS
Parker Brothers 1940's
"An Exciting Letter Game"
$6-7

HEARTS
Parker Brothers 1960
$5

"MAKE-A-MILLION"
Parker Brothers 1935
Card game
$5-7

MAKE-A-MILLION
Parker Brothers 1950's
$7-10

YAHTZEE
E.S. Lowe 1956
Similar to KISMET
"The Game That Makes Thinking...Fun!"
$5-7

YAHTZEE SCORE PADS
E.S. Lowe 1956
$3

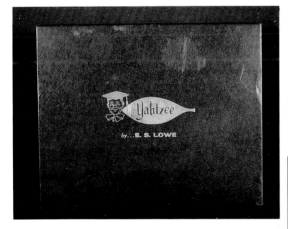

YAHTZEE
E.S. Lowe 1961
Deluxe Edition
$15-20

CHALLENGE YAHTZEE
E.S. Lowe 1974
All players score from
the same roll- has endorsement
from "The Odd Couple"
$7-9

"I'M A MILLIONAIRE"
Parker Brothers 1907
"A Laughable Game"
Card game
$5-7

TOURING

Famous and Immensely Popular Automobile Card Game. Players race their cars cross-country, with punctures, out-of-gas, and other mishaps to keep excitement and hilarity at fever pitch! Price, 75c.

ROOK The Game of Games

Loved by Millions for its unique fascination, fun and charm. Always and everywhere popular! Including rules for "ONE HIGH" ROOK. New editions, with smart, crisp narrow cards. Price, 75c.

FLINCH

Now selling in its 8th million. A Great Standard **Card** Game for over a generation. Always popular—always a Best Seller! 150 cards. Price, $1.00.

PIT Great Fun Making Game

For Laughter, Excitement, and a general Good Time, **PIT** has no rival! For a child's party, one of the merriest amusements conceivable! Price, 75c.

PIT
Parker Brothers 1919
Card game
"Bull and Bear Edition"
$5-10

PIT
Parker Brothers 1920's
John Held Jr cover
$15-20

PIT
Parker Brothers 1930's
$5

PIT
Parker Brothers 1930's
$5

PIT
Parker Brothers 1947
$5-6

PIT
Parker Brothers 1950's
$5-7

PIT
Parker Brothers 1973
W/Trading Bell
$5-7

TOURING
Parker Brothers 1926
Improved Edition
Card game
$5-7

TOURING
Parker Brothers 1955
$5

TOURING
Parker Brothers 1958
$5-7

TOURING
Parker Brothers 1965
$3

TOURING An original card game for all ages based on an automobile tour. It may be played by two to four players singly, or as partners. Punctures and out of gas mix with good roads and mileage. Complete the tour to win. 99 cards boxed.

PIT Fun, laughter and excitement for three to seven players. PIT is different from any other card game and has no rival as a fun maker. All ages enjoy it. Bull & bear cards add to the fun. For a party game it has no equal as an icebreaker.

ROOK Always and everywhere a favorite card game. Loved for its unique and exciting play. Cards are of the finest quality and there are rules for a number of other copyright games, and one solitaire. The greatest of all home games.

FLINCH One of the best known and most popular card games. Its play is quite different from other card games but it is easy to learn and fun for all ages. Pack contains 150 cards, with modern faces and backs, packed in a handsome box.

94

FLINCH
Flinch Card Co 1913
Card Game
$5-10

FLINCH
Flinch Card Co 1935
$6-9

FLINCH
Parker Brothers 1938
New Edition
$5-7

FLINCH
Parker Brothers 1940's
$5

FLINCH
Parker Brothers 1940's
$5

FLINCH
Parker Brothers 1940's
$5

FLINCH
Parker Brothers 1951
$5

FLINCH
Parker Brothers 1963
$4

ROOK
Rook Card Co 1924
Card game
$7

ROOK
Parker Brothers 1920's
$7

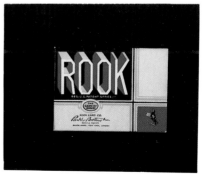

ROOK
Parker Brothers 1936
$5

95

W. H. SCHAPER
PRESIDENT

REE RON

Chapter 5

W.H. Schaper

W. H. Schaper was a Minneapolis mailman who liked to whittle fishing lures as he walked along his route. One day, while designing a new type of bait, he drew several legs and a head on the "creature" he had drawn. The *Cootie* was born.

Actually, the Cootie was born much earlier. World War One Doughboys found themselves in trenches infested with lice, and named the pesky insects "cooties." Early paper and pencil games evolved from the idea of the imaginary bug, and in 1939 Transogram printed a game called COOTIE "based on the old favorite" in which players tried to place bits of wood parts onto a drawing of a two dimensional body. But in 1948, encouraged by friends who liked the little bug "Herb" Schaper had created, he took his total savings of $75.00 and set up shop in his already crowded basement. He then created the plastic bug that kids loved to take apart. Although it started as a toy, by 1949 the plastic Cootie evolved into a game, and Herb's net capital had soared to $1,400.00. By 1950 he had sold more than 1,200,000 COOTIE games and had added several more kinds of games to his repertoire. The Cootie empire was established.

Herb Schaper's ability to sense which games would be a hit was always on target. He developed STADIUM CHECKERS from an idea a man dreamed up while sitting in a football stadium, and SKUNK was developed from an older game. A notable lapse in judgement occurred when he turned down a word game he was offered in 1953. That game was SCRABBLE.

From an interview in 1976, William Garrity, Schaper Manufacturing's president, said "Schaper stumbled into a marketing situation created by a vacuum in the industry at the time. For a long while toys were considered to be for children who lacked minimal reading skills. The prevailing theory of the time stated that kids weren't supposed to start playing with games until they were six or seven. The game of COOTIE bridged that gap because it was a game for kids aged three to five, required very little explanation and could be played with members of their peer group. Parents reacted positively because they were beginning to become conscious of the need for introducing younger children to the social disciplines, such as sharing or taking turns. COOTIE happened at the right time to bridge the gap. COOTIE sold for more than twenty years without any changes to the product, and the only changes made (a slightly more modern face and larger parts) occurred because the original dies were wearing out and had to be replaced anyway."

The lure of COOTIE and TICKLE BEE, TUMBLE BUG and STADIUM CHECKERS is in their use of plastics. Their very design harkens back to a more innocent time when the properties of plastics materials were just being discovered. Crude yet colorful, they succeeded in being more than just a game; they were fun toys, too.

While most collectors have little interest in Schaper games, I find them aesthetically very pleasing. Something nostalgic is in their minimalist packaging designs of crew-cut boys or pig-tailed girls. The shiny plastic bespeaks a simpler time when America was more innocent. Every Schaper game was even "Sanitary Wrapped," whatever that meant.

Schaper continued to design toys and games, and the company went public in 1961. In 1965, Schaper purchased the St. Croix Corporation, and Schaper itself was bought by Kusan in 1971. In 1976, this entity acquired Cosom, and in 1986 the Schaper Company was purchased by Tyco Toys. W. H. Schaper died in September, 1980.

Schaper games include:

COOTIE
DELUXE COOTIE
TRICKY TRASH TRUCK
GIANT COOTIE GAME AND BANK
HUMPTY DUMPTY
JACK BE NIMBLE
LONDON BRIDGE
RUB A DUB TUB
BILLY GOAT
DON'T SPILL THE BEANS
THE LAST STRAW
ANTS IN THE PANTS
DON'T BLOW YOUR TOP
DON'T BREAK THE ICE
CAT IN THE BAG
TIDDLE TAC TOE
PUT 'N TAKE
TUMBLE BUG
LI'L STINKER
SHAKE BINGO
TICKLE BEE
SKUNK
CASPER THE FRIENDLY GHOST
STADIUM CHECKERS
SOMBRERO
MONEY CARD
OPTILE
LETTER PILE
AIR TRAFFIC CONTROLLER
WHIRLY BIRD
TWIZZLE
FINDERS KEEPERS
BUTTON FACTORY
DAMBLOCKS
TIPPY TEEPEE
SOK-O
DUNCE
MILL
CORRAL
STAGECOACH
MAGNETIC CAR RACE
THING DING
MAGNETIC MAILMAN

PIG IN THE GARDEN
NIBBLES 'N BITES
COOTIE HOUSE
WHO YOU?
PULL THE RUG OUT
VOODOO DOLL GAME
DON'T COOK YOUR GOOSE
KING OF THE HILL
PEEK-A-BOO
HUFF & PUFF
HAVE A HEART
MOON BLAST OFF
CLEAN SWEEP
BIG MOUTH
HOP*POP
DON'T GO OVERBOARD
PUCK LUCK HOCKEY
BANGO! BANGO!
SHIFTY GEAR
TUB-A-DUB
INCH WORM
YE OLDE FISHIN HOLE
SNAP-EZE
TURTLE GAME
TWENTY QUESTIONS
TOLL CAR
HORSE PLAY
BLACK BALL EXPRESS
CHICKEN
SQUARES
MONKEYS & COCONUTS
PICKIN'
SCARECROW
SPARE-TIME BOWLING
LONDON BRIDGE
WING-IT
ROLL A WAY DERBY
PENNY PINCHER
SHAKE A LEG
THE PUZZLING PYRAMID
KICKBACK
TILT SCORE
I'M GEORGE GOBEL AND HERE'S THE GAME

COOTIE PARTY GAME
Unique Novelty Co-1920's
Based on "Flapper" dress and
"Charleston" pose I'd imagine
this game is from the 1920's
Probably one of several kinds
of paper and pencil COOTIE Games
$15-20

COOTIE
Transogram 1939
"New and Exciting Way to Play
an Old Favorite"- Instead of
simply checking off on paper
a leg or body when the
appropriate dice number is
rolled, in this game you placed
wooden eyes, antennae, body or
legs over the matching picture
$15-25

COOTIE
Transogram 1939
$15-25

THE GAME OF COOTIE
Schaper 1949
Roll the dice and put together
plastic pieces that form a
"Cootie" bug- This cover design
was used for many years, and this
game is very common
$12-20

DELUXE 6 COOTIE
Schaper 1950's
Larger box contained
6 "Cooties" rather than 4
$20-25

THE GAME OF COOTIE
Schaper late 1950's
$10-15

COOTIE
Schaper 1960's
$7-10

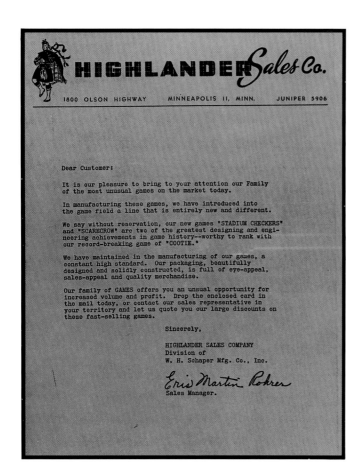

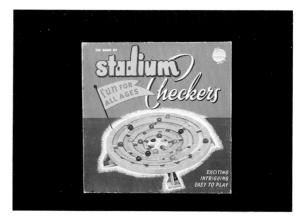

THE GAME OF STADIUM CHECKERS
Schaper 1952
Object is to turn nested plastic
rings so that marbles will fall
into hole at bottom.
$7-10

Highlander Sales Company handled the marketing
of Schaper's games in the beginning, and this
letter heralds the introduction of Schaper's 2nd and
3rd games after **COOTIE**; **SCARECROW** and **STADIUM
CHECKERS** They are modestly described
as "two of the greatest designing and engineering achievements
in game history".

STADIUM CHECKERS
Schaper 1960's
$5-8

LI'L STINKER GAME
Schaper 1956
"Played like Old Maid"
with plastic tiles
$5-7

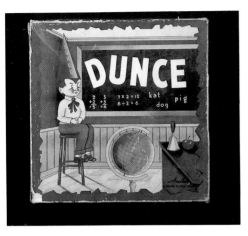

DUNCE
Schaper 1955
"The Old Game of Ghosts"
Played like HANGMAN, or alternately,
like COOTIE or
SCARECROW, substituting a
little boy.
$12-15

LET'S PLAY DUNCE
Schaper late 1950's
$8-10

STAGECOACH
Schaper 1958
Track game, kind of
unusual for Schaper
$18-20

SHAKE BINGO
Schaper 1960's
Bingo game using dice
$5-7

BANGO! BANGO!
Schaper 1960's
Object of game is
to smack edge of plastic
with enclosed sticks "Just
Right" to propel marble
into home base
$15-20

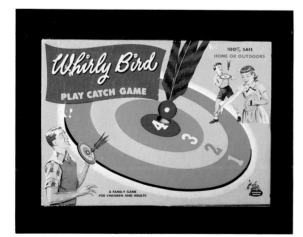

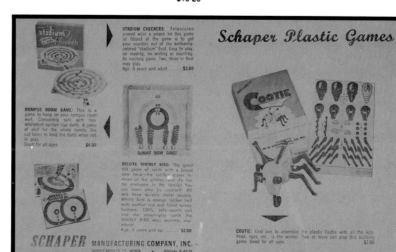

WHIRLY BIRD PLAY CATCH GAME
Schaper 1958
Rubber darts are caught
on bullseye shield
$12-15

CLEAN SWEEP
Schaper 1967
Mothers of America must have loved this quintessential
Schaper game; a spring loaded "Garbage Can"
exploded a million bits of "Trash" onto the game board
(and presumably the floor). Players had to sweep the
good trash into their respective corner. A Marvin Glass design.

WHO YOU? GAME
Schaper 1968
Animal Charades-
Marvin Glass design
$13-15

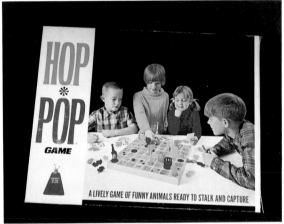

HOP*POP GAME
Schaper 1968
Big plastic animals
Marvin Glass design
$15-18

HUFF 'N PUFF GAME
Schaper 1968
Spring loaded wolf
came out and smashed
your house- have you
ever seen such excited
looking kids?
$12-15

PULL THE RUG OUT GAME
Schaper 1968
Kind of hopeless game in which
you try to "pull the rug out"
from under a bunch of teneously
balanced objects
$12-15

THE TWIZZLE GAME
Schaper late 1950's
Neat game where you
aim a marble down a spherical
mound at the pop up score you
want to get
$10-12

TILT SCORE
Schaper 1964
Tilting marble maze game
$10-15

BLACK BALL EXPRESS
Schaper 1957
Marble track game
$10-12

THE GAME OF CHICKEN
Schaper 1957
Similar to SHAKE BINGO
$5-7

TUMBLE BUG
Schaper 1950's
Oddly weighted "bugs" are
released from a starting gate
and tumble down a ramp to the
finish
$18-20

THE PUZZLING PYRAMID
Schaper 1959
Using a magnetic wand,
you maneuver a metal ball
through a maze up the
side of the Pyramid into
the hole in top
$8-12

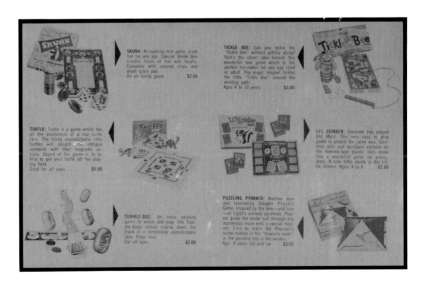

Ad shows the famous TICKLE BEE, everyone's
favorite game from childhood.

THING DING
Schaper 1960's
Using the THING DING Machine, you try
to build a mechanical man, woman, child
dog, cat or bird. Marvin Glass design.

CLEAN SWEEP
Schaper 1967
$25-35

KICK BACK
Schaper 1965
Plastic horses kick
a ball back and forth
$5-8

MONKEYS AND COCONUTS
Schaper 1965
$10-14

I'M GEORGE GOBEL AND HERE'S THE GAME
Schaper 1955
Track game based on personalilty
George Gobel- Object is to produce
a T.V. show- Unusual for Schaper to
be associated with this kind of game
$20-30

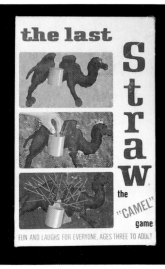

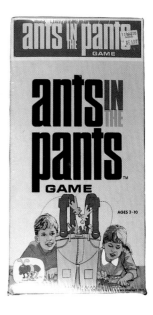

THE LAST STRAW
Schaper 1966
"The 'Camel' Game"
If you overload the
Camel's baskets with
straw you "break" his
back
$7-10

PUT & TAKE GAME
Schaper 1965
Betting game using
teetotum (top-like spinner)
$5-7

SKUNK
Schaper 1968
Roll the special
dice but don't get
"Skunked"
$4-7

ANTS IN THE PANTS
Schaper 1970
Flip "Ants" into a
big pair of plastic
overalls-Marvin Glass design
$5-8

ANTS IN THE PANTS
Schaper 1976
$3-5

MOON BLAST OFF
Schaper 1970
"The Winners Blast Off
for Earth Below, the Loser
Doesn't Get to Go"- and
presumably dies on the Moon-
Marvin Glass design
$15-20

THING DING
Schaper 1960's
$25-35

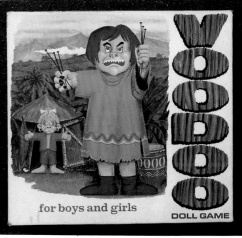

DON'T GO OVERBOARD
Schaper 1971
Don't let your plastic
men fall off the ship
$5-7

MONEY CARD
Schaper 1972
"An American Express Travel Game"
Use your AMEX card to travel
through Europe-Unusual
$15-20

VOODOO DOLL GAME
Schaper 1967
Scary game in which a
Witch Doctor would spring
from a thatched hut if you
stuck the wrong pin in-
$20-27

AIR TRAFFIC CONTROLLER GAME
Schaper 1974
"Be the First to Land Your Planes
Safely"
$12-17
From the collection of Jeffrey Lowe.

Chapter 6

Entertainment

In creating the all encompassing category "entertainment," games that have some link with television, movies or any other media influence have been included. In most cases there were not enough examples to sustain a separate chapter for each (unlike western and military games) or they were not of an unusual enough nature (as are bookshelf games) to justify an entire category. There are a few subcategories that warrant a mention.

Games involving monsters became popular in the 1960s due to the popularity of Aurora's monster models, which were in turn inspired by Universal Studios' monster movies of the 1930s and 1940s which were being dumped into television as this new medium's voracious need for products developed. Other games relating to monsters or scary stuff also have been included to keep the theme going.

Walt Disney's Mickey Mouse and friends have generated an enormous amount of merchandise over the years, including many games, a few of which are represented here.

Cartoons, in the form of animated characters created for television or movies, and characters from comic books and comic strips have been included in this category, many coming from well-established lineages extending from the 1930s and beyond. The 1960s in particular introduced a host of memorable cartoon characters, many created by the animation studio of Hanna-Barbera.

Board games based on game shows are here, as well as drama, comedy or adventure shows. Some games based on outer space themes were popular in the 1950s and 1960s, so they and their resulting milieu are displayed.

The following are games born of entertainment...

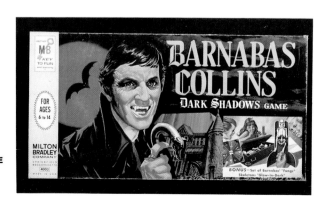

BARNABAS COLLINS DARK SHADOWS GAME
Milton Bradley 1969
$25-35

MONSTER OLD MAID
Milton Bradley 1964
"Monster Size Cards"
$15-25

WOLFMAN MYSTERY GAME
Hasbro 1963
From a series of "Monster" mystery games, inspired by the
Aurora Monster Models of the time. Almost all the covers
featured moody, abstract art. The actual games were
not too scary.

THE OUTER LIMITS GAME
Milton Bradley 1964
Based on the T.V. series
$100-150

JOURNEY TO THE UNKNOWN GAME
Remco 1968
Based on the obscure T.V.
show
$75-95
Courtesy of Toy Scouts, Inc.

DARK SHADOWS GAME
Whitman 1968
Based on the ABC Soap Opera-
Large play mat with playing cards
$20-30

THE TWILIGHT ZONE GAME
Ideal 1964
$75-100
Courtesy of Rick Polizzi.

FRANKENSTEIN MYSTERY GAME
Hasbro 1963
"Find the Lurking Monster"
$100-125

DRACULA MYSTERY GAME
Hasbro 1963
$100-125

WOLFMAN MYSTERY GAME
Hasbro 1963
$100-125

THE CREATURE FROM THE BLACK LAGOON MYSTERY GAME
Hasbro 1963
"Enter the Depths of the Black Lagoon"-
In addition, THE PHANTOM OF THE OPERA MYSTERY
GAME was created for this series
$125-175

GODZILLA GAME
Ideal 1964
Based on the movie monster
$100-150
Courtesy of Toy Scouts, Inc.

GODZILLA GAME
Mattel 1978
The monster strikes at
your passing space ships
$20-25

KING KONG GAME
Milton Bradley 1966
Based on the animated series
$15-25

KING KONG
Ideal 1976
Based on the re-make of
the original movie
$15-20

KING KONG GAME
Ideal 1963
Based on the movie monster
$75-110
Courtesy of Toy Scouts, Inc.

HEXED
Tryne Games 1960
Puzzle game
$3-5

MYSTIC SKULL
Ideal 1964
"The Game of Voodoo"
Marvin Glass design
$25-40

WEIRD-OHS GAME
Ideal 1964
Based on toy characters
$75-95
Courtesy of Rick Polizzi.

WHICH WITCH?
Milton Bradley 1970's
3-D game takes you through
a haunted house-Marvin Glass
design
$20-25

CREATURE CASTLE GAME
Whitman 1979
Card game
$10-12

GHOSTS!
Milton Bradley 1985
"Creepy, Sneaky Guess Who
Game"
$7-9

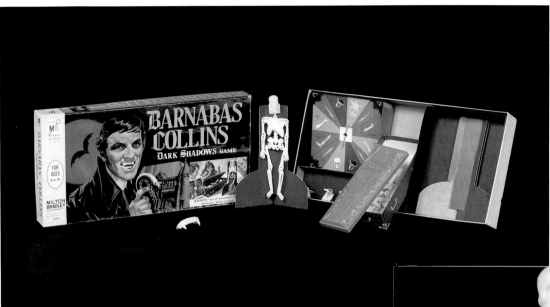

BARNABAS COLLINS DARK SHADOWS GAME
Milton Bradley 1969
Based on the ABC daytime Soap Opera about monsters living in a small town. HANGMAN, in essence. You built a skeleton bone by bone with pieces from a coffin. The winner got to wear the included fangs. Everything glowed in the dark.

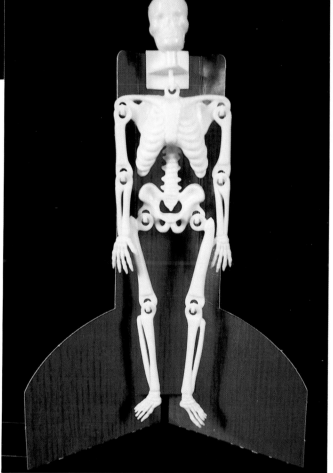

SUPERSTITION
Milton Bradley 1977
An obstacle course of danger to the Wizard's tomb
$12-18

MOSTLY GHOSTLY!
Cadaco 1975
"And All Fun!"-Similar to
BARNABAS COLLINS-Glow in the dark bones
$12-18

MYSTERY MANSION
Milton Bradley 1984
3-D game with a "Secret Behind Every Door"
$8-10

SPACE PILOT
Cadaco-Ellis 1951
Beautiful, elaborate game
$35-55
From the collection of Jeffrey Lowe.

CAPTAIN VIDEO
Milton Bradley 1950
Very early T.V. series game
$50-65
Courtesy of Rick Polizzi.

SPACE CHASE
United Nations Constructors Inc 1967
Similar to COUNTDOWN
$20-25

ORBIT
Parker Brothers 1959
$25-35
Courtesy of Rick Polizzi.

SPACE GAME
Parker Brothers 1953
"A Race for Treasure"
$25-45
From the collection of Jeffrey Lowe.

MEN INTO SPACE
Milton Bradley 1960
Based on the T.V. series
$25-35
Courtesy of Rick Polizzi.

BLAST OFF!
Selchow & Righter 1953
"The Moving Planet Space Game"
$30-40
From the collection of Jeffrey Lowe.

SPACE RACE GAME
Built-Rite 1960's
Small track game
$10

BLAST-OFF!
Waddington 1969
"The Game of Modern
Space Exploration"
$25-35
From the collection of Jeffrey Lowe.

APOLLO A VOYAGE TO THE MOON
Tracianne 1969
Includes "Moon Rocks"
$15-20

COUNTDOWN
E.S. Lowe 1967
Astronaut cards,
plastic and wooden rockets
$20-25

ZAXXON
Milton Bradley 1982
Based on the arcade
game by Sega
$7-9

PAC-MAN GAME
Milton Bradley 1980
Marble game based on the
arcade game
$7-10

PAC-MAN CARD GAME
Milton Bradley 1982
Based on the arcade
game
$5-7

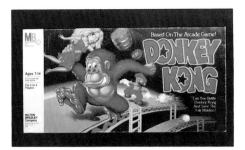

DONKEY KONG
Milton Bradley 1981
Based on the arcade game
$8-10

POPEYE
Parker Brothers 1983
Based on the arcade game
$5-7

TURBO
Milton Bradley 1981
Based on the arcade game
by Sega
$5- 7

GARFIELD
Parker Brothers 1981
Based on the comic-strip cat
$5-7

ADVENTURES OF POPEYE GAME
Transogram 1957
Based on the comic-strip hero
$35-55

MANDRAKE THE MAGICIAN GAME
Transogram 1966
Based on the comic-strip
character
$25-35

THE PHANTOM RULER OF THE JUNGLE GAME
Transogram 1966
Based on the comic-strip hero-Came with
clay and skull ring to leave "imprints"
$35-75
Courtesy of Rick Polizzi.

BUCK ROGERS GAME
Transogram 1960's
"Adventures in the 25th
Century"-Based on the
comic strip personality
$25-30
Courtesy of Rick Polizzi.

BUCK ROGERS GAME
Milton Bradley 1979
Based on the T.V. series
$10-15

LI'L ABNER HIS GAME
Milton Bradley 1949
Based on the comic-strip
$35-45
Courtesy of Toy Scouts, Inc.

THE LI'L ABNER GAME
Parker Brothers 1969
Based on the comic strip
$15-25
Courtesy of Toy Scouts, Inc.

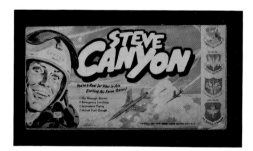

STEVE CANYON
Lowell 1959
Based on the comic-strip
character
$25-45

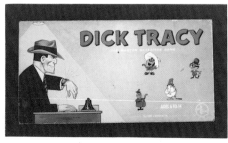

DICK TRACY THE MASTER DETECTIVE GAME
Selchow & Righter 1961
Based on the animated T.V. series
$25-35

DICK TRACY CRIME STOPPER
Ideal 1963
$35-50

COMIC CARD GAME
Milton Bradley 1972
Oversized playing cards
of famous comic-strip
characters
$12-19

DICK TRACY CRIME STOPPER
Ideal 1963
Large, CONCENTRATION-like game based on the animated T.V. series of the time. "Finds Leads, Decodes Clues, Solves Crime".

THE NEW FANTASTIC FOUR GAME
Milton Bradley 1978
"Featuring Herbie the Robot"
3-D game by Marvel Comics
$10-13

DUDLEY DO-RIGHT'S FIND SNIDELY GAME
Whitman 1976
Based on the cartoon
characters
$10-14
From the collection of Jeffrey Lowe.

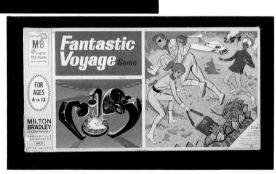

UNDERDOG TO THE RESCUE GAME
Whitman 1975
Based on the cartoon character
$10-12

JONNY QUEST GAME
Transogram 1964
Based on the great animated
T.V. series
$45-75
Courtesy of Rick Polizzi.

THE MONSTER SQUAD GAME
Milton Bradley 1977
Based on the T.V. series
$15-19

FANTASTIC VOYAGE GAME
Milton Bradley 1968
Based on the animated T.V.
series which was based on
the movie
$20-25

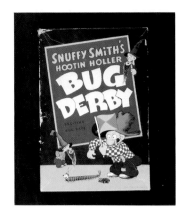

FLASH GORDON GAME
Game Gems 1965
Based on the comic strip
hero- Scarce game
$45-55

SNUFFY SMITH'S HOOTIN HOLLER BUG DERBY
Jaymar 1950's
"Exciting Bug Race"
Based on the comic strip character-
From a game series- Another box version
exists
$15-20

THE ARCHIE GAME
Whitman 1969
From the animated T.V.
series
$25-30

BLONDIE AND DAGWOOD'S RACE FOR THE OFFICE GAME
Jaymar 1950
Based on the comic strip characters-
Same series as SNUFFY SMITH
$20

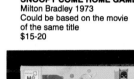

PEANUTS
Selchow & Righter 1959
"The Game of Charlie Brown and
His Pals"
Based on the comic strip
$20-25
From the collection of Jeffrey Lowe.

LUCY'S TEA PARTY GAME
Milton Bradley 1971
Large game with plastic
tea cups-Based on the
comic strip character
$15-20
From the collection of Jeffrey Lowe.

SNOOPY COME HOME GAME
Milton Bradley 1973
Could be based on the movie
of the same title
$15-20

SNOOPY'S DOGHOUSE GAME
Milton Bradley 1977
Plastic dog houses
Based on the comic strip dog
$10-15
From the collection of Jeffrey Lowe.

CALLING SUPERMAN
Transogram 1954
Based on the super hero
$45-65
Courtesy of Rick Polizzi.

BATMAN GAME
Milton Bradley 1966
Based on the super hero-
Common game
$25-35

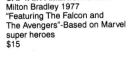

CAPTAIN AMERICA GAME
Milton Bradley 1977
"Featuring The Falcon and
The Avengers"-Based on Marvel
super heroes
$15

THE INCREDIBLE HULK GAME
Milton Bradley 1978
"With the Fantastic Four"
There was a Spider-Man game
as well- Based on the Marvel
super heroes
$10-15

CASPER THE FRIENDLY GHOST GAME
Milton Bradley 1959/1960's
Based on the animated character-
Excruciatingly common game
$10-13

THE FLINTSTONES GAME
Milton Bradley 1971
Based on cartoon characters
$10-15

THE JETSONS FUN PAD GAME
Milton Bradley 1963
$35-45

DASTARDLY AND MUTTLEY IN THEIR FLYING MACHINES
Milton Bradley 1970
Based on the cartoon characters
$15-18

CAPTAIN CAVEMAN AND THE TEEN ANGELS GAME
Milton Bradley 1980
Based on the animated series
$10-13

CASPER ELECTRONIC ADVENTURE GAME
Tarco 1962
"Develop Your Coordination"
Based on cartoon character
$20-25
Courtesy of Toy Scouts, Inc.

PEBBLES FLINTSTONE GAME
Transogram 1962
Based on animated family's baby
$35-46

THE JETSONS GAME
Milton Bradley 1985
Based on animated family
$8-10

THE WACKY RACES GAME
Milton Bradley 1969
Based on cartoon series
$20-25
Courtesy of Rick Polizzi.

TOM AND JERRY GAME
Milton Bradley 1968
Based on the animated
characters
$15-19

THE FLINTSTONES STONEAGE GAME
Transogram 1961
"The Game That Rocked Bedrock!"
Based on the animated characters
$20-30

THE FLINTSTONES PRESENT DINO THE DINOSAUR
Transogram 1961
Based on cartoon family's
pet dinosaur
$25-45

INSPECTOR GADGET GAME
Milton Bradley 1983
Based on animated T.V. series
$5-7

THE NEW ADVENTURES OF GILLIGAN
Milton Bradley 1974
Based on animated series-
3-D playing board
$20

TOM AND JERRY GAME
Milton Bradley 1977
Here's how to date a game-
This game is identical to the
1968 version- But that version
has a diagonal strip in the
lower right hand corner. That
generally means the game is
from somewhere in the mid to
late 1960's. This game has no
strip and is from 1977
$10

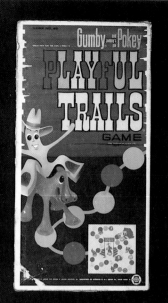

PLAYFUL TRAILS GAME
Lakeside 1968
"Gumby and Gumby's Pal Pokey"
Based on animated characters
$35-45

THE JETSONS FUN PAD GAME
Milton Bradley 1963
Based on the animated T.V. series. A
balancing game utilizing plastic space ships. Similar
to THE GAME OF YERTLE.

BULLWINKLE HIDE 'N SEEK GAME
Milton Bradley 1961
Based on animated T.V. series
$25-45

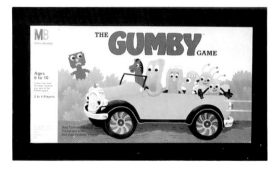

JUMPING DJ SURPRISE ACTION GAME
Mattel 1962
Beany and Cecil- Spring loaded
DJ (Dishonest John) would jump up
at inappropriate moments
$25-37
Courtesy of Rick Polizzi.

THE GUMBY GAME
Milton Bradley 1988
Based on animated characters
$10

MILTON THE MONSTER GAME
Milton Bradley 1966
Based on animated T.V. series
$20-30
Courtesy of Rick Polizzi.

QUICK DRAW McGRAW PRIVATE EYE GAME
Milton Bradley 1960
Based on cartoon characters
$20-25

SCOOBY-DOO AND SCRAPPY-DOO GAME
Milton Bradley 1983
Based on animated characters
$10

RICHIE RICH
Milton Bradley 1982
Based on comic book character
$10

HUCKLEBERRY HOUND
Milton Bradley 1981
 Based on cartoon
character
$10

HUCKLEBERRY HOUND "BUMPS" GAME
Transogram 1961
Based on animated characters
$20-25

YOGI BEAR GAME
Milton Bradley 1971
Based on cartoon character
$10-15

YOGI BEAR PRESENTS SNAGGLEPUSS FUN AT THE PICNIC GAME
Transogram 1961
 Based on cartoon characters
$25-30

ROAD RUNNER GAME
Milton Bradley 1968
Based on cartoon characters
$25

THE ROAD RUNNER GAME
Whitman 1969
"Beep-Beep! Outrace Wile E. Coyote"
Based on animated characters
$20-25

SPEED BUGGY GAME
Milton Bradley 1973
Based on animated T.V. series
$10-15

THE HAIR BEAR BUNCH GAME
Milton Bradley 1971
Based on animated T.V. series
$15-18

THE GREAT GRAPE APE GAME
Milton Bradley 1975
Based on animated series
3-D board
$12-17

FANGFACE
Parker Brothers 1979
 Based on the animated series
$10-15

SEALAB 2020 GAME
Milton Bradley 1973
Based on the animated T.V. series
$15-20

BATTLE OF THE PLANETS GAME
Milton Bradley 1979
Based on the Japanese animated
series
$10

THE SMURF GAME
Milton Bradley 1981
Based on animated characters-
3-D game series is still
being manufactured
$10-15

PINK PANTHER GAME
Warren 1977
Based on the animated series
$20

THE PINK PANTHER
Cadaco 1981
Based on the animated series
$7-9

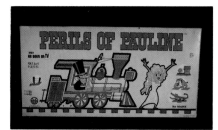

PERILS OF PAULINE
Marx 1964
 Based on the T.V. series-
Big plastic pieces- Marvin
Glass design
$45-55

THE ZANY ZOO ADVENTURES OF TENNESSEE TUXEDO GAME
Transogram 1963
Based on cartoon series
$55-65
Courtesy of Toy Scouts, Inc.

WALLY GATOR GAME
Transogram 1962
Based on animated T.V. series
$25-35

LINUS THE LIONHEARTED UPROARIOUS GAME
Transogram 1965
Game based on the animated T.V. series
$45-55
Courtesy of Toy Scouts, Inc.

TOUCHE' TURTLE GAME
Transogram 1962
Based on the cartoon character
$25-35
Courtesy of Rick Polizzi.

HASHIMOTO-SAN GAME
Transogram 1963
Based on cartoon characters
from the Hector Heathcote T.V. show
$25-35

SILLY SIDNEY THE ABSENT-MINDED ELEPHANT GAME
Transogram 1963
Based on animated character
from the Hector Heathcote show
$25-37

CAP'N CRUNCH ISLAND ADVENTURE GAME
Warren 1980's
Based on the cereal character
$8-10

CHOO-CHOO CHARLIE GAME
Milton Bradley 1960's
Based on Good and Plenty
Candy mascot
$20-25
Courtesy of Toy Scouts, Inc.

BURGER KING CHAMPIONSHIP CHECKERS
Burger King 1988
 Commemorative Limited Edition
Guinness Book of World Records
Challenge
$5

THE McDONALD'S GAME
Milton Bradley 1975
Based on the fast-food chain
$20

THE MILLERS OUTPOST GAME
Millers Outpost 1976
Based on the clothing store
$10-12

HAWAIIAN PUNCH GAME
Mattel 1978
Based on fruit drink mascot-
"If Your Opponent Lands on Your
Space You get to Squash his Pineapple!"
$10-15
From the collection of Jeffrey Lowe.

117

CAMEL THE GAME
RJRTC 1992
Dice game promo based on
cigarette
$5-8

CRACKER JACK TOY SURPRISE GAME
Milton Bradley 1976
Based on candy treat-
Came with boxes and toy surprises
$15-20

KING ZOR THE DINOSAUR GAME
Ideal 1962
Based on Ideal toy
$65-100

THE BARBIE GAME
Mattel 1960
"Queen of the Prom"
Based on popular doll from Mattel
$20-25

HOT WHEELS WIPE-OUT RACE GAME
Mattel 1968
Based on toy cars from Mattel
$20-25

POLAROID'S PARTY PACK
Polaroid 1969
"Games and Fun with a
Polaroid Land Camera"
$10-15

CHEVYLAND SWEEPSTAKES
Milton Bradley 1968
May have been promo from
dealers-Featured 1969
Corvette, Camaro, Impala Convertible,
Impala Sedan and Biscayne
$20-25

MR. MACHINE GAME
Ideal 1961
$45-75

BARBIE'S KEYS TO FAME GAME
Mattel 1963
Based on doll
$25-35

UNCLE MILTON'S EXCITING ANT FARM GAME
Uncle Milton Industries 1969
Based on popular distraction-
Loads of plastic ants
$20-25

DOMINO'S PIZZA DELIVERY GAME
Wortquest USA Inc 1989
Game based on pizza product
$10

WHERE'S THE BEEF?
Milton Bradley 1984
Based on Wendy's advertising-
Jack Davis cover
$5-9

"MATCHBOX" TRAFFIC GAME
Fred Bronner Corp 1968
Based on popular toys-
Included 2 "Matchbox" cars
$25-35

BARBIE'S LITTLE SISTER SKIPPER GAME
Mattel 1964
Based on Mattel doll
$25-30

POWER LORDS BOARD GAME
Warren 1983
"The Extra-Terrestrial Warriors"
Based on plastic toy figures
$10-15

MR. MACHINE GAME
Ideal 1961
Based on "America's Favorite Toy", the
first toy design hit by Marvin Glass. Object
of the game was to be the first to get your miniature
Mr. Machine to the toy factory.

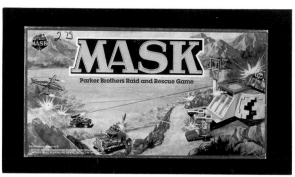

MASK
Parker Brothers 1985
Based on toy and T.V. series
$5

KEWPIE DOLL GAME
Parker Brothers 1963
Based on characters created
by Rose O'Neill
$25-30

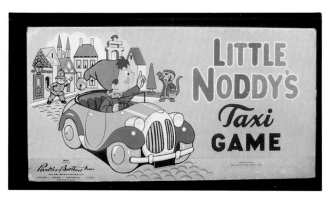

LITTLE NODDY'S TAXI GAME
Parker Brothers 1956
Based on characters created
by Enid Blyton- There is
another game in this series
$25-35
Courtesy of Rick Polizzi.

JACK AND THE BEANSTALK ADVENTURE GAME
Transogram 1957
Based on children's story
$15-20
From the collection of Jeffrey Lowe.

TRAVEL WITH WOODY WOODPECKER
Cadaco-Ellis 1956
Elaborate travel game based on
cartoon character
$20-30

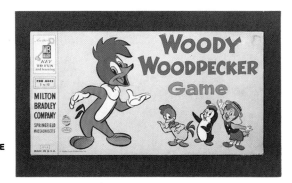

WOODY WOODPECKER GAME
Milton Bradley 1958
Based on cartoon character
$15-20

ROBIN HOOD AND HIS MERRY MEN OF SHERWOOD FOREST
Harett-Gilmer Inc 1955
Based on literary characters-
Includes gold coins
$25-30
From the collection of Jeffrey Lowe.

THE ADVENTURES OF ROBIN HOOD
Bettye-B 1956
Based on T.V. series starring
Richard Greene
$35-45
From the collection of Jeffrey Lowe.

THE REAL GHOSTBUSTERS GAME
Milton Bradley 1984
Based on animated series-
Game identical to WHICH WITCH?
$10

TARZAN TO THE RESCUE GAME
Milton Bradley 1977
Based on literary character
$15

THREE MUSKETEERS
Milton Bradley 1950
Strategy game
$15-20

THE GAME OF BLACK BEAUTY
Transogram 1958
Based on the book
$10-15

THE NANCY DREW MYSTERY GAME
Parker Brothers 1957
Based on children's literary heroine
$15-20
From the collection of Jeffrey Lowe.

THE NANCY DREW MYSTERY GAME
Parker Brothers 1959
$12-15

HOLLY HOBBIE WISHING WELL GAME
Parker Brothers 1976
Based on greeting card character-
"With Love From Parker Brothers"
$10

WALT DISNEY'S HARDY BOYS TREASURE GAME
Parker Brothers 1957
Based on children's literary heroes
$17-25
From the collection of Jeffrey Lowe.

THE HARDY BOYS GAME
Milton Bradley 1978
Based on animated series
$15-20
From the collection of Jeffrey Lowe.

THE BARON MUNCHAUSEN GAME
Parker Brothers 1933
Dice game based on literary
character adapted to radio
$10-15

THE CASE OF THE ELUSIVE ASSASSIN
Ideal 1967
$25-35

MURDER ON THE ORIENT EXPRESS
Ideal 1967
"A Sherlock Holmes Mystery Game"-
Famous Mystery Classic Series-
Based on Sir Arthur Conan Doyle's
character
$25-35
From the collection of Jeffrey Lowe.

FU MANCHU'S HIDDEN HOARD
Ideal 1967
"A Doctor Fu Manchu Mystery Game"
Famous Mystery Classic Series
Based on characters created
by Sax Rohmer
$35-45

THE CASE OF THE ELUSIVE ASSASSIN
Ideal 1967
From the "Famous Mystery Classic Series", this
game featured Ellery Queen. Elaborate styling and
strategy made all these adaptations exciting.

CHERRY AMES' NURSING GAME
Parker Brothers 1959
Based on the children's books
$25

RAGGEDY ANN'S MAGIC PEBBLE GAME
Milton Bradley 1941
Based on the popular characters
$25-35
From the collection of Jeffrey Lowe.

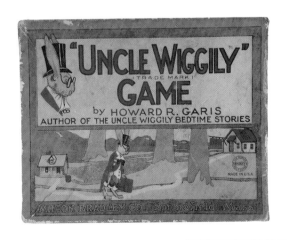

"UNCLE WIGGILY" GAME
Milton Bradley 1920's
(Shown without board)
Based on characters created
by Howard R. Garis
$25-35

RAGGEDY ANN
Milton Bradley 1954
"A Little Folks Game"
$15-18

UNCLE WIGGILY GAME
Milton Bradley 1954
$15

THE BOBBSEY TWINS ON THE FARM GAME
Milton Bradley 1957
Based on children's literary
characters
$15-20

THE MY FAIR LADY GAME
Standard Toykraft 1960's
Based on the "Hit Musical of the
Century"
$20-22

"HOW TO SUCCEED IN BUSINESS WITHOUT REALLY TRYING"
Milton Bradley 1963
Based on the play of the same name
$20

CHITTY-CHITTY-BANG-BANG GAME
Milton Bradley 1968
Based on the movie
$20-23

THE GAME OF THE WIZARD OF OZ
Whitman 1939
Based on the movie
$25-35

OFF TO SEE THE WIZARD GAME
Milton Bradley 1968
Based on the cartoon series
$20-25

RETURN TO OZ GAME
Golden 1985
Based on Walt Disney Pictures
movie- A Cadaco WIZARD OF OZ
game exists
$10

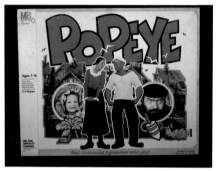

POPEYE
Milton Bradley 1980
Based on the movie
$10

UNIVERSE
Parker Brothers 1967
$20-25

ANNIE
Parker Brothers 1981
"Path to Happiness Game"
Based on movie
$5-7

AROUND THE WORLD IN 80 DAYS TRAVEL GAME
Transogram 1957
Based on the star-studded movie
$20-30

GREASE
Milton Bradley 1978
Based on the movie
$12-15

THE STING GAME
Ideal 1976
Elaborate game based on
the movie
$15-18

ESCAPE FROM NEW YORK THE GAME
TSR 1980
Simulation game based on movie
$10-12

3 MEN ON A HORSE
Milton Bradley 1936
Based on the Warner Brothers
"Laff Hit!"
$25-45

THE SECRET OF NIMH GAME
Whitman 1982
Based on the animated movie
$10

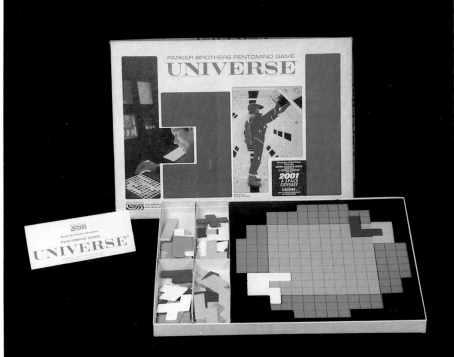

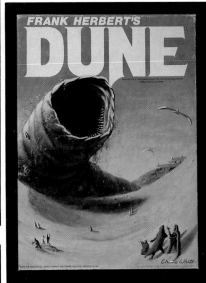

DUNE
Avalon Hill 1979
Based on Frank Herbert's book
$10

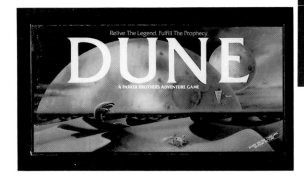

TERMINATOR 2 JUDGMENT DAY
Milton Bradley 1990's
Based on the movie starring Arnold
$10

THE GAME OF JAWS
Ideal 1975
Based on the block-buster
film- Big plastic
$15-20

DUNE
Parker Brothers 1984
Based on the movie
$15-17

ALIENS
Leading Edge Games 1986
Based on movie sequel-
Additional pewter playing pieces
were available for this
role-playing game
$10-15

ALIEN GAME
Kenner 1979
Based on movie- Cover shows
desirable Kenner Alien toy
$15-20

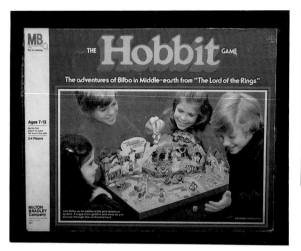

E.T. THE EXTRA-TERRESTRIAL
Parker Brothers 1982
Based on the 2nd highest grossing
film of all time
$7-9

THE HOBBIT GAME
Milton Bradley 1978
$15

RAIDERS OF THE LOST ARK GAME
Kenner 1981
Based on the movie
$10

CLASH OF THE TITANS GAME
Whitman 1981
Based on the Ray Harryhausen film
$10-12

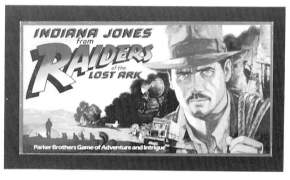

INDIANA JONES FROM RAIDERS OF THE LOST ARK
Parker Brothers 1982
Based on the movie
$12-14

SINBAD
Cadaco 1978
Based on the Ray Harryhausen
"Sinbad" movies
$20-25
From the collection of Jeffrey Lowe.

CLOSE ENCOUNTERS OF THE THIRD KIND
Parker Brothers 1978
Based on the film
$10-13

"GOODBYE, MR. CHIPS" GAME
Parker Brothers 1969
Based on the movie
$20-25

VOYAGE OF FEAR GAME
Whitman 1979
Based on the Walt Disney Production
The Black Hole
$15-17

THE HOBBIT GAME
Milton Bradley 1978
Based on Ralph Bakshi's animated film of the
famous novel "Lord of the Rings". The game is
a 3- dimensional romp through "Middle-Earth".

THE BLACK HOLE SPACE ALERT GAME
Whitman 1979
Another game based on the movie
$10

KRULL
Parker Brothers 1983
Based on the film
$12-15

125

JAMES BOND SECRET AGENT 007 GAME
Milton Bradley 1964
Based on the movie character-
This generic agent face appeared
before licensing was secured for
Sean Connery's visage
$20-25

JAMES BOND 007 THUNDERBALL GAME
Milton Bradley 1965
Based on the movie
$25-45

JAMES BOND MESSAGE FROM M GAME
Ideal 1966
The grand-daddy of all James Bond
games-Big plastic-Marvin Glass design
$75-100

STAR WARS DESTROY DEATH STAR GAME
Kenner 1978
Based on "Star Wars"
$15-20

STAR WARS YODA THE JEDI MASTER GAME
Kenner 1981
Based on "The Empire Strikes Back"-
A "Star Wars Adventures of R2-D2 Game" exists
$10-12
From the collection of Jeffrey Lowe.

JAMES BOND SECRET AGENT 007 GAME
Milton Bradley 1964
Version with Sean Connery
$20-22

GOLDFINGER JAMES BOND 007 GAME
Milton Bradley 1966
Based on the movie
$45-65

STAR WARS ESCAPE FROM DEATH STAR GAME
Kenner 1977
Based on "Star Wars"
$10

STAR WARS GAME
?-1970's-1980's?
Foreign game based on movie
$20

STAR WARS BATTLE AT SARLACC'S PIT GAME
Parker Brothers 1983
Based on "Return of the Jedi"
$10-13

ENTER THE DANGEROUS WORLD OF JAMES BOND 007
Milton Bradley 1965
Casino game based on movie
character
$15-20

JAMES BOND 007 CARD GAME
Milton Bradley 1964
Based on the movie character
Scarce
$20-25
Courtesy of Rick Polizzi.

STAR WARS
Parker Brothers 1982
Based on movies-
$20-25

STAR WARS HOTH ICE PLANET ADVENTURE GAME
Kenner 1977
Based on "The Empire Strikes Back"
$10-12

STAR WARS WICKET THE EWOK
Parker Brothers 1983
Based on "Return of the Jedi"
$8-9

WALT DISNEY'S TOMMOROWLAND ROCKET TO THE MOON GAME
Parker Brothers 1956
$25-35
Courtesy of Rick Polizzi.

DISNEYLAND MONORAIL GAME
Parker Brothers 1960
$20-25

WALT DISNEY'S OFFICIAL FRONTIERLAND GAME
Parker Brothers 1955
$15-20

WALT DISNEY'S ADVENTURELAND GAME
Parker Brothers 1956
$20-25

DISNEYLAND MONORAIL GAME
Parker Brothers 1960's
$17-20

WALT DISNEY'S OFFICIAL DAVY CROCKETT FRONTIERLAND GAME
Parker Brothers 1955
$25-35
Courtesy of Rick Polizzi.

WALT DISNEY'S FANTASYLAND GAME
Parker Brothers 1950's/1960's
$20-27

DISNEYLAND "IT'S A SMALL WORLD" GAME
Parker Brothers 1965
$15-20

DISNEYLAND RIVERBOAT GAME
Parker Brothers 1960's
$17-20

DISNEYLAND PIRATES OF THE CARIBBEAN GAME
Parker Brothers 1965
$20

WALT DISNEY'S PETER PAN
Transogram 1953
Based on the movie
$25-30
From the collection of Jeffrey Lowe.

WALT DISNEY PRESENTS SLEEPING BEAUTY GAME
Parker Brothers 1958
Based on the movie
$20-25

WALT DISNEY'S CINDERELLA GAME
Parker Brothers 1963
Based on the movie
$15-20

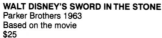

WALT DISNEY'S SWORD IN THE STONE
Parker Brothers 1963
Based on the movie
$25

WALT DISNEY PRODUCTIONS ROBIN HOOD GAME
Parker Brothers 1973
Based on the movie
$12-15

127

WALT DISNEY'S MARY POPPINS GAME
Whitman 1964
Based on the movie.
One of several games with
the "New Magic Whirl Merry-Go-Round Spinner".

WALT DISNEY'S PINOCCHIO GAME
Whitman 1962
Based on the movie
$17-20

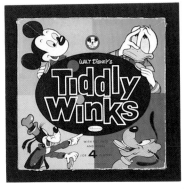

WALT DISNEY'S TIDDLY WINKS
Whitman 1963
Mickey Mouse Club
$5-7

WALT DISNEY PRESENTS PINOCCHIO GAME
Parker Brothers 1971
$10

PIN THE NOSE ON WALT DISNEY'S PINOCCHIO
Parker Brothers 1939
Large game- From the movie
$55-95
From the collection of Jeffrey Lowe.

WALT DISNEY WORLD HAUNTED MANSION GAME
Lakeside 1980's
3-D game from Florida attraction
$20-25

WALT DISNEY WORLD 20,000 LEAGUES UNDER THE SEA GAME
Lakeside 1980's
Plastic boats
$15-18

WALT DISNEY'S MARY POPPINS GAME
Whitman 1964
$20-25

WALT DISNEY'S MARY POPPINS CAROUSEL GAME
Parker Brothers 1964
Based on the film
$15-20

WALT DISNEY'S WINNIE THE POOH GAME
Parker Brothers 1964
Based on the films
$20

WALT DISNEY'S DISNEYLAND GAME
Whitman 1965
Featuring "Magic Whirl" spinner
$25-30
Courtesy of Rick Polizzi.

WALT DISNEY'S DISNEYLAND GAME
Transogram 1950's
The "New Park, as Seen on TV and
in the Movies"
$20-25

WALT DISNEY'S BABES IN TOYLAND
Parker Brothers 1961
Based on the film
$20-25
From the collection of Jeffrey Lowe.

WALT DISNEY'S WINNIE THE POOH GAME
Parker Brothers 1979
$5-7

WALT DISNEY'S BABES IN TOYLAND GAME
Whitman 1961
Based on the film
$25-35
From the collection of Jeffrey Lowe.

WALT DISNEY'S ZORRO GAME
Parker Brothers 1966
Based on the films
$20-25
Courtesy of Toy Scouts, Inc.

WALT DISNEY'S WONDERFUL WORLD OF COLOR
Parker Brothers 1962
"Professor Ludwig Von Drake Presents"-
"A Game Based on the TV Program"
$25-35
From the collection of Jeffrey Lowe.

ZORRO GAME
Whitman 1965
Based on the Disney films
$15-20

WALT DISNEY'S LUDWIG VON DRAKE TIDDLY WINKS
Whitman 1961
$5-7

THE OFFICIAL NEW YORK WORLD'S FAIR GAME
Milton Bradley 1965
Based on the 1964-1965 event
$25

THE MISS AMERICA PAGEANT GAME
Parker Brothers 1974
Based on the event
$15-20
From the collection of Jeffrey Lowe.

RUBIK'S RACE
Ideal 1982
Based on the phenomenal fad
$7-9

EMILY POST POPULARITY GAME
Selchow & Righter 1970
Based on etiquette personality-
"Win a Circle of Friends"
$15-18
From the collection of Jeffrey Lowe.

THE HARLEM GLOBETROTTERS GAME
Milton Bradley 1971
Based on animated series
$15-20
From the collection of Jeffrey Lowe.

SEE NEW YORK 'ROUND THE TOWN GAME
Transogram 1964
Based on the city
$20-25
From the collection of Jeffrey Lowe.

FLIP-IT JACKPOT
Aurora 1973
$20-25

MELVIN PURVIS' "G"-MEN DETECTIVE GAME
Parker Brothers 1930's
Based on "Former Ace of the Department
of Justice"
$35-45
From the collection of Jeffrey Lowe.

THE ULTIMATE TRIVIA GAME
Quizviz 1984
Promo for Newsweek magazine
$5-7

PEOPLE WEEKLY
Parker Brothers 1984
Trivia game based on the magazine
$5-8

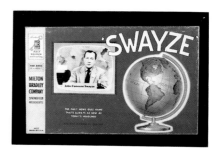

'SWAYZE'
Milton Bradley 1954
News quiz game based on T.V.
personality John CameronSwayze
$22-25

BOAKE CARTER'S GAME STAR REPORTER
Parker Brothers 1937
Based on famous news reporter
$40-50
From the collection of Jeffrey Lowe.

LARRY HARMON'S BOZO
Parker Brothers 1960's
"The World's Most Famous Clown Game"
$15-20
From the collection of Jeffrey Lowe.

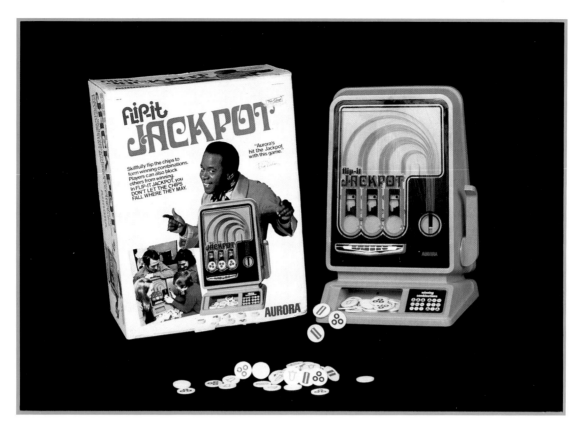

FLIP-IT JACKPOT
Aurora 1973
Endorsed by Television personality Flip Wilson.
Large game where you "flipped" chips into
correct combinations to win the jackpot.

EDDIE CANTOR'S GAME
Parker Brothers 1950's
"Tell it to the Judge"
$20-25

EDDIE CANTOR'S AUTOMOBILE GAME "TELL IT TO THE JUDGE"
Parker Brothers 1930's
$20-30

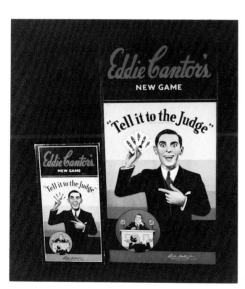

EDDIE CANTOR'S NEW GAME "TELL IT TO THE JUDGE"
Parker Brothers 1936
$30-45

TWIGGY
Milton Bradley 1967
Based on the "Queen of Mod"
$25-35
Courtesy of Rick Polizzi.

KATE SMITH'S OWN GAME AMERICA
Toy Creations 1940's
Based on personality-All
proceeds from game went to charity
$35-55

HOWDY DOODY'S T.V. GAME
Milton Bradley 1953
"A Visit to Howdy's Own T.V. Studio"
$35-40
Courtesy of Rick Polizzi.

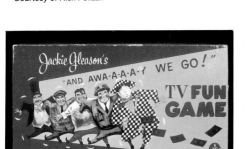

JACKIE GLEASON'S "AND AWA-A-A-A-Y WE GO!" TV FUN GAME
Transogram 1956
Based on comedian
$35-55
Courtesy of Rick Polizzi.

STORY STAGE
VIP Corp 1955
"Starring Jackie Gleason and
his TV Troupe"- Featuring the
new "Magic Magnet Character Animator"
$35-45

THE SONS OF HERCULES GAME
Milton Bradley 1966
Based on movies
$25-35

THE ALLEN FUNT CANDID CAMERA GAME
Lowell 1963
Based on T.V. show
$25-30

THE MAD MAGAZINE GAME
Parker Brothers 1979
Created by the magazine
$5-7

"SCREWBALL" A MAD MAD GAME
Transogram 1958
Revised cover-Original looked
too much like Mad's mascot-
Lawsuit threat caused cover change
$25-35
Courtesy of Rick Polizzi.

CROSS UP
Milton Bradley 1974
Crossword game- Lucille Ball
on cover
$7-10

CASEY JONES GAME BOX
Saalfield 1959
Alan Hale on cover
$20-25
From the collection of Jeffrey Lowe.

**THE ORIGINAL LITTLE RASCALS
CLUBHOUSE BINGO**
Gabriel 1958
Based on the characters
$15-20

RED SKELTON'S "I DOOD IT!"
Zondine Game Co 1947
Based on the "Radio" star
$45-65

MARLIN PERKINS' ZOO PARADE
Cadaco-Ellis 1955
Based on T.V. personality
$35-45
From the collection of Jeffrey Lowe.

MARLIN PERKINS' WILD KINGDOM GAME
Don Meier Productions 1977
$10-12

ALFRED HITCHCOCK WHY MYSTERY GAME
Milton Bradley 1967
$15

EDDIE CANTOR'S AUTOMOBILE GAME "TELL IT TO THE JUDGE"
Parker Brothers 1930's
Many versions of this popular track game endorsed by
comedian Eddie Cantor were manufactured. Players
sped around the board trying to avoid a confrontation with
"The Judge".

THE BEATLES FLIP YOUR WIG GAME
Milton Bradley 1964
The only game based on the "Fab Four"
$35-55
Courtesy of Rick Polizzi.

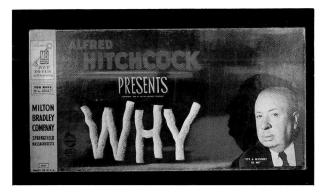

ALFRED HITCHCOCK PRESENTS WHY
Milton Bradley 1958
CLUE-like game based on film director
$25

DURAN DURAN GAME
Milton Bradley 1985
"Into the Arena"-Well made
game with tons of stuff relating
to the music group
$15-20

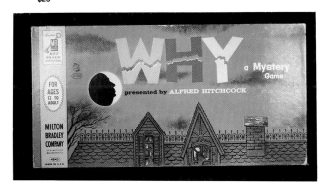

WHY
Milton Bradley 1961
"A Mystery Game Presented by Alfred Hitchcock"
$20

K-TEL SUPERSTAR GAME
K-Tel International 1973
Mail order game with plastic
gold albums and a real 45 RPM record
$15-18

133

KRESKIN'S ESP
Milton Bradley 1966
$12-15

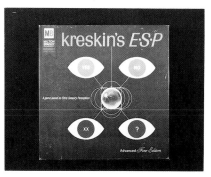

KRESKIN'S E.S.P.
Milton Bradley 1967
Advanced Fine Edition
$15-18

THE AMAZING DUNNINGER MIND READING GAME
Hasbro 1967
Mind reading personality
$20-25

MIND OVER MATTER
Ideal 1967
"The Great Julian Presents"
Another ESP game
$20-27
From the collection of Jeffrey Lowe.

MADAME PLANCHETTE HOROSCOPE GAME
Selchow & Righter 1967
Fortune telling game
$15-20

NEMO
Creston Industries 1969
"Unlock the Secrets of the Future"
$12-15

TOUCH
Parker Brothers 1970
Palmistry game
$10-12

PREDICTION ROD
Parker Brothers 1970
"Combines Divining Rod with
Lodestone to Produce Psychomagnetic
Results"
$15-17

BEWITCH
Selchow & Righter 1964
"The Game of 'Mind Reading'"
Perhaps the game that started it all?
$15-23
From the collection of Jeffrey Lowe.

JEANE DIXON'S GAME OF DESTINY
Milton Bradley 1968
Famous predictionist's astrology game
$15-20

KA-BALA
Transogram 1967
Fortune telling game that
"Glows in the Dark"
$40-65

KRESKIN'S ESP AND ADVANCED EDITION
Milton Bradley 1966 and 1967
An array of mind reading, mystical and ESP
paraphernalia. Presumably, you graduated to the
Advanced Fine Edition when you had exhausted
all the tests in the Standard Edition. A wave
of other "ESP" type games followed.

THE MERRY GAME OF FIBBER McGEE
Milton Bradley 1940
"And the Wistful Vista Mystery"
Based on radio personalities
$15-20

BURR TILLSTROM'S KUKLA AND OLLIE A GAME
Parker Brothers 1962
Based on the NBC T.V. program-No Fran
$22-25

BING CROSBY'S GAME CALL ME LUCKY
Parker Brothers 1954
Based on singer
$15-20

ALLAN SHERMAN'S CAMP GRANADA GAME
Milton Bradley 1965
Inspired by comedic fad song-
Lots of rubber bugs
$20-27

JIMMY THE GREEK ODDS MAKER POKER-DICE
Aurora 1974
Endorsed by famous bookie
$8-10

THE GAME OF YERTLE
Revell 1960
"By Dr. Seuss"-
Loads of plastic turtles
$35-55

BLUFF
Saalfield 1963
Based on political personalities
$20-25

ELECTION '68
Createk 1967
Political game
$25

DEAR ABBY GAME
Ideal 1972
Based on columnist-
Similar to SCRUPLES
$12-15

NEW FRONTIER
Colorful Products Inc 1962
"The Game Nobody Can Win"-
Game critical of Kennedy administration
$20-28
From the collection of Jeffrey Lowe.

THE EXCITING NEW GAME OF THE KENNEDYS
Transco 1962
Based on Kennedy family
$20-30
Courtesy of Rick Polizzi.

HENDRIK VAN LOON'S WIDE WORLD GAME
Parker Brothers 1933
(Shown without board)
Travel game based on famous author
$15-25

W.C. FIELDS HOW TO WIN* AT BRIDGE
The Game Keepers 1972
"*Cheat"-Another game showed
how to win at poker, using
the same methods
$7-10

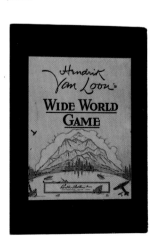

HENDRIK VAN LOON'S WIDE WORLD GAME
Parker Brothers 1933
$35-45

LARRY HAGMAN PRESENTS FLIP OUT
Mattel 1985
Endorsed by Dallas' Larry Hagman
$5

ART LINKLETTER'S HOUSE PARTY GAME
Whitman 1968
Based on television show starring Art Linkletter.
Elaborate game filled with weird things to do to
win money and prizes.

ART LINKLETTER'S GAME OF "PEOPLE ARE FUNNY"
Whitman 1954
Based on the T.V. and
radio show
$15-20

ART LINKLETTER'S HOUSE PARTY GAME
Whitman 1968
$17-20

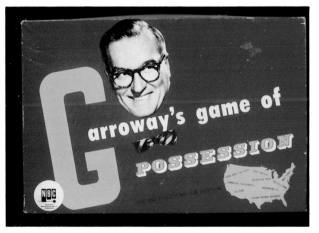

GARROWAY'S GAME OF POSSESSION
Reco 1955
Endorsed by T.V. personality Dave
Garroway
$25-35
Courtesy of Rick Polizzi.

J. FRED MUGGS 'ROUND THE WORLD GAME
Gabriel 1955
Based on chimp from Today T.V. show
$40-50
Courtesy of Rick Polizzi.

KING TUT'S GAME
Cadaco 1977
Game of Senet (game inspired
by traveling King Tut exhibit
$7-10

137

CONCENTRATION
Milton Bradley 1958
$15-20

CONCENTRATION GAME
Milton Bradley 1960
Based on the game show- 3rd Edition
$7

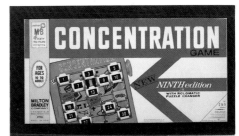

CONCENTRATION GAME
Milton Bradley 1964
9th Edition
$5

SEVEN KEYS
Ideal 1961
Based on the game show
$15-20
From the collection of Jeffrey Lowe.

P D Q
Milton Bradley 1965
"TV Game of Secret Letters"
$10-12

BY THE NUMBERS
Milton Bradley 1962
Obscure T.V. game show
$10-15

TIC-TAC DOUGH TV QUIZ GAME
Transogram 1950's
Game show with Jack Barry
$20-22

EYE GUESS
Milton Bradley 1966
Bill Cullen's T.V. game-
2nd Edition
$6-9

YOU DON'T SAY GAME
Milton Bradley 1969
Based on the NBC T.V. game
$8-10

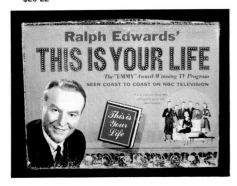

RALPH EDWARDS' THIS IS YOUR LIFE
Lowell 1950's
Emmy Award-winning T.V. program
$25-35
Courtesy of Rick Polizzi.

PASSWORD
Milton Bradley 1963
Fine Edition
$10-12

CONCENTRATION
Milton Bradley 1958
Original Edition. Based on the NBC game show.
The "Rolomatic" game board was adapted to
many other games.

PASSWORD
Milton Bradley 1962
Original Edition
Based on the game show
$7-10

PASSWORD
Milton Bradley 1963
Volume 3-The cartoon changed
$5

PASSWORD
Milton Bradley 1964
Volume 5-the caption
changed, ad infinitum
$2-3

PASSWORD
Milton Bradley 1963
Collector's Edition
$15-20

CHIT CHAT
Milton Bradley 1960's
"Hugh Downs Game of Conversation"
$7-10

JAN MURRAY'S CHARGE ACCOUNT TV WORD GAME
Lowell 1961
Based on game show
$20-25

JAN MURRAY'S TREASURE HUNT
Gardner Games 1950's
As seen on NBC
$20-22

BREAK THE BANK
Bettye-B 1955
Series 2-Game show
hosted by Bert Parks
$20-25

TO TELL THE TRUTH
Lowell 1957
Based on the game show
$25-30
Courtesy of Rick Polizzi.

PLAY YOUR HUNCH
Transogram 1960
T.V.'s "Popular Guessing Game"
$22-25

SAY WHEN!!
Parker Brothers 1961
Based on the NBC T.V. program
$20-22

2 FOR THE MONEY
Hasbro 1955
CBS game show
$20-25
Courtesy of Rick Polizzi.

MASQUERADE PARTY
Bettye-B 1955
Bizarre game show
$25-35
From the collection of Jeffrey Lowe.

REVLON'S $64,000 QUESTION QUIZ GAME
Lowell 1955
Scandal tainted game show
$25

REVLON'S $64,000 QUESTION JUNIOR QUIZ
Lowell 1955
Small-fry version
$15-20
From the collection of Jeffrey Lowe.

WHAT'S MY LINE?
Lowell 1955
Based on television's "Award Winning Panel Show".
Came with blinders, black and white photos of
strange people and a neat plastic "T.V.".

"FAMILY FEUD"
Milton Bradley 1977
Based on the game show
$5-10

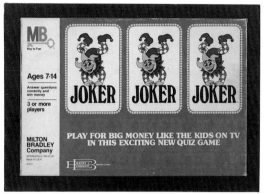

JOKER JOKER JOKER
Milton Bradley 1979
Children's quiz show
$5

TV JACKPOT GAME
Milton Bradley 1975
"As Seen on TV"-We'll have
to take their word for it
$10

THE $10,000 PYRAMID GAME
Milton Bradley 1974
Based on the T.V. game show
$7

THE HOLLYWOOD SQUARES
Whitman 1967
Elephant Graveyard of T.V.
$10-15

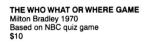

THE WHO WHAT OR WHERE GAME
Milton Bradley 1970
Based on NBC quiz game
$10

NAME THAT TUNE GAME
Milton Bradley 1957
Game show hosted by George De Witt
$20-24

NAME THAT TUNE GAME
Milton Bradley 1959
2nd Edition-Came with
33 1/3 record
$15

DREAM HOUSE TV HOME GAME
Milton Bradley 1968
As seen on ABC
$15-17

MAKE A FACE
Milton Bradley 1962
First Edition
$20

CAMOUFLAGE
Milton Bradley 1961
T.V. game with "Plastic Screen"
to put over home T.V. screen
$15-20

VIDEO VILLAGE
Milton Bradley 1960
Very popular game based
on the CBS program
$25-30

THE PRICE IS RIGHT
Lowell 1958
$25-35

BID IT RIGHT
Milton Bradley 1964
Card game based on T.V.
game show The Price Is Right
$10-12

DOUBLE EXPOSURE
Ideal 1961
Based on CBS program
$20

I'VE GOT A SECRET
Lowell 1956
T.V. show hosted by Garry Moore
$20-25
Courtesy of Rick Polizzi.

MERV GRIFFIN'S WORD FOR WORD GAME
Mattel 1963
Based on the popular NBC T.V. show. Players
at home had to beat the "Gyro-Timer" in a race
to unscramble words.

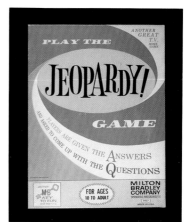

JEOPARDY!
Milton Bradley 1964
Based on the T.V. show
$15

THE NEWLYWED GAME
Hasbro 1967
Original Edition
Based on the ABC show
$10

THE NEWLYWED GAME
Chuck Barris Productions 1979
$10

MATCH GAME
Milton Bradley 1974
Again based on the game show
$8-10

THE NEWLYWED GAME
Hasbro 1969
3rd Edition-"Lovable Game" series Based on the Popular T.V. show
$5

THE MATCH GAME
Milton Bradley 1963
Based on the game show
$15-17

CALL MY BLUFF
Milton Bradley 1965
Based on T.V. game show
$10-15
Courtesy of Rick Polizzi.

143

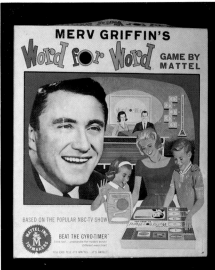

BEAT THE CLOCK
Lowell 1954
Based on the famous CBS game show hosted by
Bud Collyer and the fabulous "Roxanne".
"40 hilarious, laugh provoking stunts" were
included in this home game, which was the
first game show game produced by Lowell. Sylvania
was the sponsor.

NUMBER PLEASE
Parker Brothers 1961
Based on the ABC program
hosted by Bud Collyer
$12-15

PERSONALITY GAME
Milton Bradley 1968
Based on the NBC show
$15-20

QUIZ KIDS OWN GAME BOX
Parker Brothers 1940
Popular radio program
$20

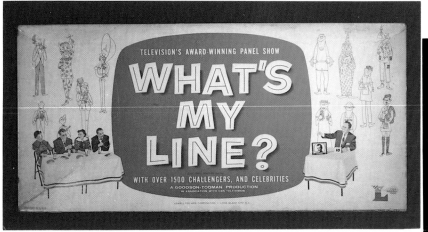

WHAT'S MY LINE?
Lowell 1955
$25-35

STUMP THE STARS
Ideal 1962
Based on "Charades"-
Game Show on CBS
$15-25
From the collection of Jeffrey Lowe.

DOLLAR A SECOND
Lowell 1950's
Based on ABC show
hosted by Jan Murray
$20-25
From the collection of Jeffrey Lowe.

NBC-TV NEWS GAME
Dadan Inc 1962
With Chet Huntley
$25-35
From the collection of Jeffrey Lowe.

THE PRICE IS RIGHT
Lowell 1958
Home version of "TV's Fast Paced show
of Bid and Brain". Big plastic and
some really "Fiftie's" prizes.

NBC PEACOCK GAME
Selchow & Righter 1966
NBC showed off it's new color
"Peacock" in this game
$20-25
From the collection of Jeffrey Lowe.

TODAY WITH DAVE GARROWAY
Athletic Products Inc 1950's
Fantastic game based on the NBC show
$35-55
Courtesy of Rick Polizzi.

AS THE WORLD TURNS
Parker Brothers 1966
Travel game based on the soap opera
$15-20

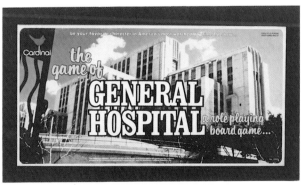

THE GAME OF GENERAL HOSPITAL
Cardinal 1982
Role playing game based on the
daytime soap opera
$10

MARY HARTMAN MARY HARTMAN
Reiss 1977
Based on the bizarre T.V. show
$10-15

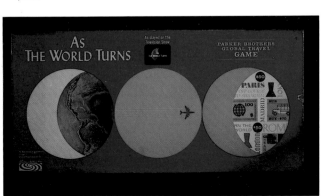

147

THE GAME OF DRAGNET
Transogram 1955
Based on the T.V. series starring
Jack Webb
$25-35

PERRY MASON CASE OF THE MISSING SUSPECT GAME
Transogram 1959
Based on T.V. show starring
Raymond Burr- Identical box as DRAGNET
$35-45

ROUTE 66 TRAVEL GAME
Transogram 1962
T.V. show with Martin Milner
and George Maharis
$45-50
Courtesy of Rick Polizzi.

THE RAT PATROL DESERT COMBAT GAME
Transogram 1967
Based on T.V. series
$45-55
Courtesy of Toy Scouts, Inc.

RIPCORD
Transogram 1962
(Game is full color)
Based on "Action-Packed"
T.V. show
$50-60
Courtesy of Toy Scouts, Inc.

SEA HUNT UNDERWATER ADVENTURE GAME
Lowell 1960
From T.V. show starring Lloyd Bridges
$45-65
Courtesy of Toy Scouts, Inc.

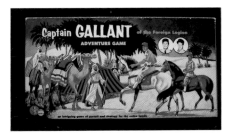

CAPTAIN GALLANT OF THE FOREIGN LEGION ADVENTURE GAME
Transogram 1955
Based on the series
$20-30
Courtesy of Rick Polizzi.

THE A-TEAM
Parker Brothers 1984
"Color Photo of B.A. Inside!"
$7-10

MR. T GAME
Milton Bradley 1983
Based on animated show
$10

KOJAK THE STAKEOUT DETECTIVE GAME
Milton Bradley 1975
T.V. series starring Telly Savalas
$15-18

BARETTA THE STREET DETECTIVE GAME
Milton Bradley 1976
Starring Robert Blake
$10-13

STARSKY & HUTCH DETECTIVE GAME
Milton Bradley 1977
Based on the series
$12-15

ELIOT NESS AND THE UNTOUCHABLES GAME
Transogram 1961
Based on the program starring Robert Stack
$25-45

MURDER, SHE WROTE
Warren 1985
Based on the popular T.V. show
starring Angela Lansbury
$15-18

COLUMBO DETECTIVE GAME
Milton Bradley 1973
That's Peter Falk on the
cover
$10-15

77 SUNSET STRIP
Lowell 1959
Based on the T.V. series
$30-40
Courtesy of Rick Polizzi.

MR. NOVAK GAME
Transogram 1963
"Adventures of a Young Teacher in a
Metropolitan High School". Based on
NBC series, starring James Franciscus.

T.H.E. CAT GAME
Ideal 1967
Based on the NBC series
$35-45
Courtesy of Toy Scouts, Inc.

PETER GUNN DETECTIVE GAME
Lowell 1960
T.V. show starring Craig Stevens
$40-50
Courtesy of Toy Scouts, Inc.

PHILIP MARLOWE GAME
Transogram 1960
Series starring Philip Carey
$35-45
Courtesy of Toy Scouts, Inc.

HAWAIIAN EYE
Lowell 1963
Based on the detective series
$35-45

NATIONAL VELVET GAME
Transogram 1961
T.V. series based on the movie
$20-25
From the collection of Jeffrey Lowe.

149

THE SIX MILLION DOLLAR MAN
Parker Brothers 1975
Series starring Lee Majors
$10-12

BIONIC CRISIS
Parker Brothers 1975
Based on The Six Million Dollar Man
$8-10

THE BIONIC WOMAN
Parker Brothers 1976
Series starring Lindsay Wagner
$10

LUCAN GAME
Milton Bradley 1977
Based on the "Popular TV Series"
$15-20

FANTASY ISLAND GAME
Ideal 1978
Based on the T.V. show
$10-14

THE WALTONS GAME
Milton Bradley 1974
Based on the popular show
$15-19

THE DUKES OF HAZZARD GAME
Ideal 1981
From the T.V. show starring
"The General Lee"
$10

KNIGHT RIDER
Parker Brothers 1983
"Based on the Hit TV Series"
$8-10

"CHIPS" GAME
Ideal 1981
From the series
$10

THE S.W.A.T. GAME
Milton Bradley 1976
Based on the T.V. series
$10-15

THE EMERGENCY! GAME
Milton Bradley 1973
Based on the T.V. show
$8-10

M.A.S.H. GAME
Milton Bradley 1981
From the long running series
$8-10

CHARLIE'S ANGELS GAME
Milton Bradley 1977
Based on the television series-
"Farrah" cover
$15-20

CHARLIE'S ANGELS GAME
Milton Bradley 1978
"Cheryl" cover
$10-15

MIAMI VICE THE GAME
Pepperlane Industries 1984
Big game based on the series
$15-20

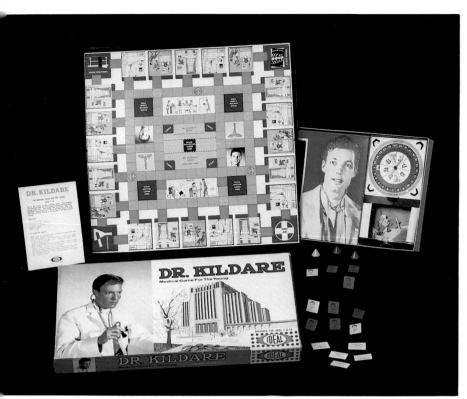

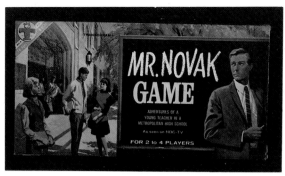

MR. NOVAK GAME
Transogram 1963
$25-35

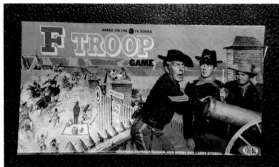

DR. KILDARE
Ideal 1962
"Medical Game for the Young". Based on the
television series starring Richard Chamberlain.
Players take turns "diagnosising" patients.

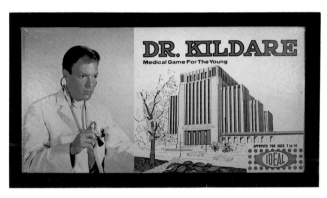

DR. KILDARE
Ideal 1962
$20-25

F TROOP GAME
Ideal 1965
Based on the comedy series
$55-65
Courtesy of Toy Scouts, Inc.

BEN CASEY M.D. GAME
Transogram 1961
Medical series starring
Vincent Edwards
$15-20

THE NURSES GAME
Ideal 1963
Based on the "True-To-Life"
television drama
$25-30

THE WACKIEST SHIP IN THE ARMY GAME
Standard Toykraft 1964
Based on the NBC T.V. comedy
$40-50
Courtesy of Toy Scouts, Inc.

GOMER PYLE GAME
Transogram 1964
Comedy series
$35-50
Courtesy of Rick Polizzi.

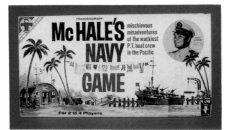

McHALE'S NAVY GAME
Transogram 1962
Starring Ernest Borgnine
$20-35
Courtesy of Rick Polizzi.

BAMBOOZLE
Milton Bradley 1962
Based on the T.V. show
"McKeever and the Colonel"
$25-35

GANG WAY FOR FUN GAME
Transogram 1964
From the "Broadside" TV show
$25-35
From the collection of Jeffrey Lowe.

LASSIE GAME
Game Gems 1965
Starring Lassie the "Wonder Dog"
$15-25

FLIPPER FLIPS
Mattel 1965
From the T.V. series
$20-25

LEAVE IT TO BEAVER AMBUSH GAME
Hasbro 1959
From a game series based on "The Beaver"
$20-30

LEAVE IT TO BEAVER ROCKET TO THE MOON SPACE GAME
Hasbro 1959
$35-45
Courtesy of Rick Polizzi.

LEAVE IT TO BEAVER MONEY MAKER GAME
Hasbro 1959
$30-35
Courtesy of Rick Polizzi.

HAPPY DAYS
Parker Brothers 1976
From the T.V. series
$10-12

THE FONZ HANGING OUT AT ARNOLDS
Milton Bradley 1976
"Platform Card Game" Based on the series
$15

LAVERNE & SHIRLEY
Parker Brothers 1977
Spin-off series from "Happy Days"
$12-15

MORK & MINDY GAME
Parker Brothers 1979
Spin-off series from "Happy Days"
$10-12

MORK & MINDY CARD GAME
Milton Bradley 1978
$7

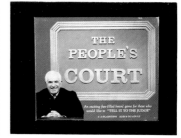

THE PEOPLE'S COURT
Hoyle Products 1986
Based on the show
$10

MARGIE THE GAME OF WHOOPEE!
Milton Bradley 1961
Based on the T.V. series
$15-20

HEE HAW
Dooley-Fant Inc 1975
Uncommon game
$10-15

BARNEY MILLER
Parker Brothers 1977
Based on the comedy series
$10

WELCOME BACK, KOTTER
Ideal 1976
Actually contains a "rubber hose"
$10-12

PATTY DUKE GAME
Milton Bradley 1963
Based on the popular series
$20-25

I DREAM OF JEANNIE GAME
Milton Bradley 1965
From the T.V. series
$25-35

THE PETTICOAT JUNCTION GAME
Standard Toykraft 1960's
Based on the series
$25-35

THE BEVERLY HILLBILLIES GAME
Standard Toykraft 1963
"If You Like the TV Show, You'll
Love the Game"
$25-35

**SET BACK THE BEVERLY HILLBILLIES CARD
GAME**
Milton Bradley 1963
$15

THE FLYING NUN GAME
Milton Bradley 1968
Sacrilegious series starring Sally Field
$20-25

CAR 54' WHERE ARE YOU?
Allison 1962
Based on the NBC comedy
$55-65
Courtesy of Toy Scouts, Inc.

MISTER ED
Parker Brothers 1962
"The Talking Horse"
$25-35

THE DICK VAN DYKE GAME
Standard Toykraft 1962
Based on the series
$65-75
Courtesy of Toy Scouts, Inc.

THE BRADY BUNCH GAME
Whitman 1973
Based on the large family
$25-35
Frcm the Collection of Daniel Wachtenheim.

THE MUPPET SHOW
Parker Brothers 1977
Based on the program
$10

THE GREEN ACRES GAME
Standard Toykraft 1965
Based on the outlandish program
$45-55
Courtesy of Toy Scouts, Inc.

THUNDERBIRDS
Parker Brothers 1967
Based on the live-action puppet series
by Gerry Anderson. The game had cards, wooden
disks and metal spaceships to travel around
the world.

GIDGET FORTUNE TELLER GAME
Milton Bradley 1966
Another game based on T.V. series
$20-25
Courtesy of Rick Polizzi.

PHIL SILVERS SGT. BILKO..
Gardner Games 1950's
From the series "You'll Never
Get Rich"
$25-35

THE LUCY SHOW GAME
Transogram 1962
Based on her second series
$35-45
Courtesy of Rick Polizzi.

THE TAMMY GAME
Ideal 1963
Based on the series
$20-25
Courtesy of Rick Polizzi.

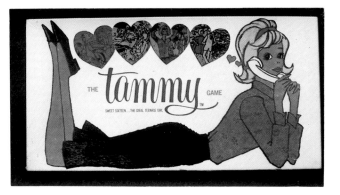

GILLIGAN'S ISLAND GAME
Game Gems 1964
Sought after game
$75-100
Courtesy of Rick Polizzi.

THE SOUPY SALES GAME
Ideal 1965
"Soupy Sez"-From the show
$25-35
Courtesy of Toy Scouts, Inc.

SOUPY SEZ GO-GO-GO!
Milton Bradley 1961
"Wow! What a Game!"
$25-45

ROMPER ROOM MAGIC TEACHER
Bar-Zim 1960's
Educational game (yeech)
$10-20

SKATEBIRDS GAME
Milton Bradley 1978
Based on the T.V. show
$10-12
From the collection of Jeffrey Lowe.

THE NEW ZOO REVUE
Ungame Co 1981
Another educational game
$7-10

H.R. PUFNSTUF GAME
Milton Bradley 1971
Based on the live action
children's show
$20
Courtesy of Rick Polizzi.

ARCHIE BUNKER'S CARD GAME
Milton Bradley 1972
From "All In the Family"
$10

THE ALL IN THE FAMILY GAME
Milton Bradley 1972
$8-10

BUNKER POKER
Cadeaux(Milton Bradley) 1972
In cigar box
$10-15

THE ADDAMS FAMILY GAME
Ideal 1965
Based on the spooky/kooky family
$45-70
Courtesy of Toy Scouts, Inc.

THE ADDAMS FAMILY CARD GAME
Milton Bradley 1965
$20-25
Courtesy of Rick Polizzi.

THE MUNSTERS CARD GAME
Milton Bradley 1964
Two cover versions exist-
$20-25
Courtesy of Rick Polizzi.
There are a lot of other games featuring The Munsters:
PICNIC GAME,DRAG RACE GAME and
MASQUERADE PARTY GAME. All are sought after.

BEWITCHED
Game Gems 1965
From the ABC series
$45-75
Courtesy of Rick Polizzi.

STYMIE CARD GAME
Milton Bradley 1964
"Inspired by the Bewitched
T.V. Series"
$20-25

MY FAVORITE MARTIAN GAME
Transogram 1963
Based on the CBS comedy
$45-75

HEY! HEY! THE MONKEES GAME
Transogram 1967
Based on the NBC series
$45-75
Courtesy of Rick Polizzi.

CAMP RUNAMUCK GAME
Ideal 1965
From the series
$25-35
From the collection of Jeffrey Lowe.

VOYAGE TO THE BOTTOM OF THE SEA GAME
Milton Bradley 1964
Based on the adventure show
$20-25

LAND OF THE LOST GAME
Milton Bradley 1975
Based on the popular show
$15-20
From the collection of Jeffrey Lowe.

THE PARTRIDGE FAMILY GAME
Milton Bradley 1971
From the series
$15-20

SIGMUND AND THE SEA MONSTERS GAME
Milton Bradley 1975
Based on the live action
children's show
$15-20

THUNDERBIRDS
Parker Brothers 1967
$35-45

THE KORG: 70,000 B.C. GAME
Milton Bradley 1974
Based on the T.V. program
$15-22

SHINDIG TEEN GAME
Remco 1965
From the music show
$35-45
Courtesy of Rick Polizzi.

ELECTRA WOMAN AND DYNAGIRL GAME
Ideal 1977
Live action heroines
$20

SUPERCAR TO THE RESCUE GAME
Milton Bradley 1962
Gerry Anderson series
$55-75

PLANET OF THE APES
Milton Bradley 1974
 Based on the T.V. series-
Marvin Glass design
$20-25

THE TIME TUNNEL SPIN-TO-WIN
Pressman 1967
$45-75
Courtesy of Toy Scouts, Inc.
A whole series of "Spin Cycle" games
were made for many T.V. shows

THE TIME TUNNEL CARD GAME
Ideal 1966
(Shown without cover)
There was a regular game as well
$35-45
Courtesy of Toy Scouts, Inc.

STAR TREK GAME
Ideal 1967
Based on the NBC series
$35-55

THE THRUSH 'RAY-GUN AFFAIR' GAME
Ideal 1966
From the television spy series The Man
From U.N.C.L.E. Large, elaborate game
with many plastic parts and the omniscient
"Ray-Gun".

LOST IN SPACE GAME
Milton Bradley 1965
Based on the outer space series
$35-50

BATTLESTAR GALACTICA
Parker Brothers 1978
"Star Wars" inspired T.V. series
$10

LOST IN SPACE 3D ACTION FUN GAME
Remco 1966
(Game exists in color)
Highly sought after game
$155-185
Courtesy of Toy Scouts, Inc.

SPACE: 1999
Milton Bradley 1976
"Adapted From the Television Series"
$15-20

JOHN DRAKE SECRET AGENT GAME
Milton Bradley 1967
Based on the action show
$25-35
Courtesy of Rick Polizzi.

157

THE MAN FROM U.N.C.L.E. CARD GAME
Milton Bradley 1965
Features Napoleon Solo
$15

THE MAN FROM U.N.C.L.E. GAME
Ideal 1965
Based on the spy series
$25-35

ILLYA KURYAKIN CARD GAME
Milton Bradley 1966
$20-25
Courtesy of Rick Polizzi.

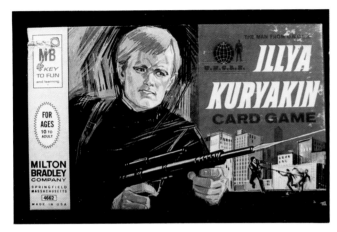

THE THRUSH 'RAY-GUN AFFAIR' GAME
Ideal 1966
$55-75

"I SPY" MINI-BOARD CARD GAME
Ideal 1966
$20

"I SPY" GAME
Ideal 1965
Based on spy show
$35-45

"GET SMART" MINI BOARD CARD GAME
Ideal 1965
$20-25
Courtesy of Toy Scouts, Inc.

"GET SMART" THE EXPLODING TIME BOMB GAME
Ideal 1965
Based on the spy comedy starring Don Adams
$40-50
Courtesy of Toy Scouts, Inc.

THE IPCRESS FILE
Milton Bradley 1966
Based on the film
$25-35
Courtesy of Rick Polizzi.

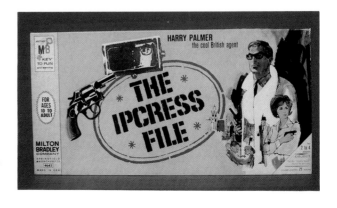

Index